Pink and Brown People

THOMAS SOWELL

Pink and Brown People

And Other Controversial Essays

HOOVER INSTITUTION PRESS
Stanford University / Stanford, California

"Black Leaders I" and "Black Leaders II" were originally published as "The Other Blacks: I. Leaders—or, 'Leaders'?" and "The Other Blacks: II. Led, and Misled" by the *New York Times*. © 1979 by the New York Times Company. Reprinted by permission. Essays from the *Washington Star*, the *Los Angeles Herald Examiner*, and the *Los Angeles Times* were reprinted by permission of the publishers.

HOOVER PRESS PUBLICATION 253

© 1981 by the Board of Trustees of the
Leland Stanford Junior University
All rights reserved
International Standard Book Number 0-8179-7532-2
Library of Congress Catalog Card Number 81-80295
Printed in the United States of America
Design by L. Ziedrich

INTRODUCTION

THESE ESSAYS DEAL WITH issues ranging from politics to race to economic policy and military defense. The newspaper columns in which they first appeared required getting to the heart of an issue without a lot of words. There was no space for elaborate build-up to a conclusion, for detours into side issues, or for masses of statistics or footnotes. But the briefness of these essays was liberating rather than restricting. It meant that the goal was simply to hit the nail on the head, not overwhelm scholarly critics with tables, graphs, and equations.

The problems dealt with here are as serious as survival and as ludicrous as the pretensions of the anointed, who want to impose their superior wisdom and virtue on the rest of us poor slobs. These two very different subjects in fact go together. The visions of the anointed are among the hazards to our survival, and especially to the survival of our freedom.

Running through these discussions of highly disparate issues is a central theme: there are very different visions of how the world works, and the opposition of these underlying visions is what causes the particular clashes that develop over energy, crime, price controls, foreign policy, and a host of other issues.

For some, the world is envisioned as a place that needs only their superior virtue and wisdom to achieve happiness and fulfillment. This might be called the vision of the anointed. To others, the problems inherent in man and the cruel choices of nature can only be imperfectly resolved, and even this modest goal requires great efforts by all, not inspired salvation by a few messiahs. This can be labeled a vision of social processes.

The institutions that bring out the cooperation of numerous and very different people—the family, the Constitution, the market, traditions— are all sacred to believers in the vision of social processes as the way to make the best of the tragic human condition. These very same institutions are often viewed as obstacles to the "solutions" prescribed in the vision of the anointed.

These essays deal with the particular battlegrounds on which these general principles are fought out, in repeated clashes between the same adversaries. Sometimes the overheated political rhetoric of our time is dealt with humorously, because recognizing nonsense for what it is, is one way of reducing the harm it can do.

Thanks are due to the *New York Times*, the *Los Angeles Herald-Examiner*, the *Los Angeles Times*, and the *Washington Star* for permission to reprint these columns. There are a few minor changes of wording from the originals, but the substance is the same as when they first appeared in print.

THOMAS SOWELL

The Hoover Institution
October 24, 1980

1

RACE AND ETHNICITY

MUCH OF WHAT IS BELIEVED about race and ethnicity is based on repetition rather than history. It would be a major undertaking to disentangle the assumptions, visions, and partial truths that make up the media picture of "minorities" and their relationship to "society" (See my *Ethnic America* [Basic Books, 1981]). The following essays simply try to puncture some of the more gross misunderstandings.

Unfortunately, major public policy commitments—from job quotas to school busing—have been made on the basis of a social vision that leaves out many uncomfortable facts and substitutes passionate assumptions. That such policies may fail is only a small part of the dangers. The vulnerability of multiracial and multiethnic societies to internal strife and dissolution is painfully apparent from history, and from despotic and bloody examples in our own time.

These essays explore some of the ways our current approaches accomplish little and endanger much. They examine the old, discredited racial beliefs and the new and more fashionable myths. These are not simply discussions of blacks and whites. The rich ethnic history of the United States provides many insights on current issues. No two groups or times are exactly alike, but the patterns that emerge again and again in history cannot be ignored. At the very least, we have to make comparisons even to discover uniqueness. It turns out that our times are not so unique as we imagine. What may be unique is our sense that we—and our "experts"—have found "the solution," when in fact we are creating new and more dangerous problems.

Pink and Brown People

THE WASHINGTON STAR / OCTOBER 6, 1977

A man who says we should really "tell it like it is" refers to whites and blacks as "pink people" and "brown people." These jarring phrases are of course more accurate, but that may be why they are jarring. Race is not an area especially noted for accuracy—or for rationality or candor. More often it is an area of symbolism, stereotype, and euphemism. The plain truth sounds off-key and even suspicious. Gross exaggerations like *white* and *black* are more like the kind of polarization we are used to. Racial classifications have always been a problem, but in the United States such attempts at neat pigeonholing become a farce, in view of the facts of history.

Less than a fourth of the "black" population of the United States is of unmixed African ancestry. And a noted social historian estimates that tens of millions of whites have at least one black ancestor somewhere in generations past. Even in the old South, where "one drop of Negro blood" was supposed to make you socially black, the actual laws required some stated fraction of black ancestry, to avoid "embarrassing" some of the "best" white families.

What all this boils down to is a wide spectrum of racial mixtures with an arbitrary dividing line and boldly contrasting labels applied to people on either side of the line. The human desire for classification is not going to be defeated by any biological facts. Those who cannot swallow pseudobiology can turn to pseudohistory as the basis for classification. Unique cultural characteristics are now supposed to neatly divide the population.

In this more modern version, the ghetto today is a unique social phenomenon—a unique problem calling for a unique solution. Many of those who talk this way just happen to have this solution with them and will make it available for a suitable combination of money and power.

Ghettos today certainly differ from white middle-class neighborhoods. But past ghettos always differed from past middle-class neighborhoods, even when both were white. Indeed, the very word *ghetto* came historically from a white minority community of people, classified by the fact that they held religious services one day earlier than others. People will classify on any basis. With today's recreation-oriented weekends, religious classifications are often based on what service you *would have* attended.

2

American ghettos have always had crime, violence, overcrowding, filth, drunkenness, bad school teaching, and worse learning. Nor are blacks historically unique even in the degree of these things. Crime and violence were much worse in the nineteenth-century slums, which were almost all white. The murder rate in Boston in the middle of the nineteenth century was about three times what it was in the middle of the twentieth century. All the black riots of the 1960s put together did not kill half as many people as were killed in one white riot in 1863.

The meaning of the term *race riot* has been watered down in recent times to include general hell raising (and posing for television) in the hell-raisers' own neighborhood. In the nineteenth century it was much uglier. Thousands of members of one "race" invaded the neighborhood of another "race"—both, typically, European—to maim, murder, and burn. Today's disorders are not in the same league, whether measured in blood or buildings.

Squalor, dirt, disease? Historically, blacks are neither first nor last in any of these categories. There were far more immigrants packed into the slums (per room or per square mile) than is the case with blacks today—not to mention the ten thousand to thirty thousand children with no home at all in nineteenth-century New York. They slept under bridges, huddled against buildings or wherever they could find some semblance of shelter from the elements.

Even in the area where many people get most emotional—educational and I.Q. test results—blacks are doing nothing that various European minorities did not do before them. As of about 1920, any number of European ethnic groups had I.Q.'s the same as or lower than the I.Q.'s of blacks today. As recently as the 1940s, there were schools on the Lower East Side of New York with academic performances lower than those of schools in Harlem.

Much of the paranoia that we talk ourselves into about race (and other things) is a result of provincialism about our own time as compared to other periods of history. Violence, poverty, and destroyed lives should never be accepted. But there is little chance of solving any problem unless we see it for what it is, not what it appears to be in the framework of reckless rhetoric.

Not a Chinaman's Chance

LOS ANGELES HERALD EXAMINER / FEBRUARY 13, 1980

Chinese-Americans are among the most prosperous Americans—and among the poorest. Chinese-Americans have more education, on the average, than whites—but also have a higher illiteracy rate than blacks. There is nothing "inscrutable" about this. It is a result of a combination of severe discrimination in the past and the more recent achievements of the Chinese people in the United States.

Among the older Chinese in this country are men who immigrated back when every form of legal discrimination, social bias, and outright violence were used against the Chinese. The phrase "not a Chinaman's chance" originated in that era to describe hopeless odds. Are the Chinese "disadvantaged"? Do they require "compensation" for the past? It all depends on how you look at it.

Many an aged Chinese-American today lives in poverty after a lifetime of working for low pay in some laundry or restaurant. At one time, those two industries employed over half the Chinese in this country. They were kept out or driven out of other work.

Perhaps worst of all, many of the aged Chinese are men who have never had a chance for a normal family life. The first immigrants from China were almost exclusively men. The U.S. government clamped down immigration restrictions before the women could join them. At one time, there were about 27 Chinese men to every Chinese woman in the United States. Most of the men lived and died in loneliness as well as poverty.

Once the Chinese were allowed any opportunity at all, they made the most of it. Today, one-fourth of all Chinese employed in the United States work in professional or scientific fields. Most of today's generation have it made.

How do you "compensate" those who never had a chance? Most of those who suffered the most are dead, many by suicide. What of the old man living out his last days in a single room somewhere in Chinatown? No amount of "preferential" treatment of Chinese applicants for college or jobs is going to do him any good.

The recent Chinese refugees are not likely to be helped much, either. Preferential treatment helps people who already have some of the qualifications needed, not people starting out at the bottom.

Affirmative action may salve the consciences of some whites, but it

4

seldom compensates those individuals who actually suffered wrongs, whether among the Chinese or among other groups. Quotas often create new injustices and breed new animosities to plague us in future years.

On what grounds can the government legitimately show preference for the Chinese over, say, the Irish? The Chinese have higher incomes and more education than the Irish. Of course, the government does not single out the Irish for discrimination. It singles out various other groups for preference. But all these various groups, including women, add up to about two-thirds of the population of the United States.

What this means is that affirmative action authorizes discrimination against one-third of the population of the country. For government contractors, it requires it. No one planned it this way. That is just the way things often work out when everyone hops on a bandwagon. We may have our hands full just trying to do justice in our own time, without trying to rewrite history.

The Death of Joe Louis

LOS ANGELES TIMES / APRIL 14, 1981

I cried at the death of a man I never saw except on a movie or television screen. It is hard to recreate for a new generation the world in which Joe Louis first appeared, or his role in changing that world for blacks in general. But to those of us who are black and old enough to remember that era, Louis had an importance that went far beyond sports.

Joe Louis came out of nowhere in 1934, when he first fought professionally, to become an overnight sensation with a series of quick knockouts of some of the best-known fighters of his time. Three years later, he was heavyweight champion of the world. For the next dozen years—longer than any other man—his fights ended with the familiar announcement, "The winner—and still champeen—Joe Louis!"

What made Louis a unique figure was not simply his great talent as an athlete. He appeared at a time in American history when blacks were not only at a low economic ebb—earning about one-third of the income of whites—but were the butt of ridicule, from the streets to the radio ("Amos 'n' Andy") to the movie screen (*Steppin' Fetchit*).

In this kind of world, Joe Louis became the most famous black man in America. What he did as a man could reinforce or counteract stereotypes that hurt and held back millions of people of his race. How he fared in the ring mattered more to black Americans than the fate of any other athlete in any other sport, before or since. *He was all we had.*

It was a heavy load to put on a 23-year-old boxer with very little education or worldly knowledge. Yet for more than a decade he carried that load with dignity, with gentlemanliness, with sportsmanship, with occasional flashes of humor—in short, with "the unbought grace of life" that was his gift. His athletic skills put him in the limelight, but it was his human qualities that made Joe Louis an idol to millions of Americans, of all racial and ethnic backgrounds.

The phrase that was applied to Louis then—and sounds so strange today—was that he was "a credit to his race." We now have the luxury of criticizing such a phrase. But many of us drew on that credit. Joe Louis was a continuing lesson to white America that black did not mean clown or lout, regardless of what the image-makers said. It was a lesson that helped open doors that had been closed too long. He also instilled pride in blacks. There were not only more black athletes because of Joe Louis; there were also more black doctors and lawyers and economists. By the

6

end of his career, people were saying that Louis was a credit to the *human* race.

As a fighter, Louis dominated boxing as no man before or since. He fought every top contender and gave rematches to anyone who made any sort of showing against him. (No one ever went the distance in a second fight with Joe Louis.) He ducked nobody, used no unsportsmanlike tactics, denigrated no one. He set a record for one-round knockouts that still stands.

Like many other fighters, Louis fought too long past his prime and let too much money get away from him. Illness and tax problems clouded some of his retirement years. But on the eve of his death, he received a standing ovation when introduced before a boxing match. He went out a winner—and still "champeen," to those of us privileged to share his era.

"Representation"—
or Misrepresentation?

LOS ANGELES HERALD EXAMINER / JULY 4, 1979

When certain ideas take hold in fashionable circles,many individuals and institutions rush toward these ideas like lemmings rushing to the sea. The great mindless idea of our time is that all groups would be equally "represented" everywhere if it were not for discrimination or other sins of "society."

A flood of words and mountains of statistics have poured out, applying this principle. But the principle itself remains almost totally unexamined. Are statistical "imbalances" or "underrepresentation" of groups so rare that we can say discrimination must be involved whenever such things appear? On the contrary, few groups of any kind are evenly represented anywhere, and lopsided percentages are commonplace.

Even at this late date in history, you would have to move the homes of 52 percent of all Americans of southern European ancestry if you wanted them to be spread evenly among Americans of northern European ancestry. Are we now going to start busing Greeks into Irish neighborhoods?

Women are just over half of the population but commit only about one-fourth of the murders or suicides. Are women going to have to step up their rate of carnage, in the name of equality?

One-fourth of all American hockey players come from one state (Minnesota). Is it really surprising that each of the 50 states (including California and Florida) doesn't provide its 2 percent of hockey players?

Half of all Mexican-American women get married in their teens, while only 10 percent of Japanese-American women get married that young. Every group has its own values and priorities, and these effect all sorts of economic and social results. That is why human beings are not randomly distributed anywhere.

Television stations keep elaborate statistics on who watches what programs because the composition of audiences is very different from one show to the next, and advertisers want to know whom they are talking to. Voting patterns, child-rearing practices, alcohol consumption, and all sorts of other voluntarily chosen activities vary enormously by education, location, religion, and numerous other factors. It can't be discrimination, because each person makes his own decisions for himself. We are not random in our behavior because we come from different backgrounds.

8

Everyone knows that there has been discrimination against some racial and ethnic groups and that it has still not been completely stamped out. We don't need pseudoscience claiming that one can measure discrimination by statistical "representation."

Even an ideally nondiscriminating society would not have an even distribution of ethnic groups in jobs, colleges, or other places. Racial and ethnic groups are very different from one another in many ways: age, fertility, regional distribution, and many other variables. Polish-Americans are a decade older than Chinese-Americans, who in turn are almost a decade older than Mexican-Americans. Age makes a big difference in income, so different ethnic groups would be earning different pay even if everything else was the same between them, and even if no employers ever had a speck of prejudice. Income differences between age brackets are even greater than income differences between blacks and whites. So are income differences among the states.

One of the driving ideas behind the school integration crusade of the past quarter of a century is that black youngsters performed poorly because they were in segregated schools. It was a reasonable theory and a humane desire to help. What was unreasonable was turning this belief into gospel, and the gospel into law. What was inhumane was disrupting children's lives over an unproven idea in vogue with the anointed.

Disparities in school performance have existed as long as there have been statistics and different groups of people. Even when all the groups were white, when all lived in the same neighborhoods, and all sat next to each other in school, different ethnic groups did not perform the same. Back before World War I, a study in New York City showed that German and Jewish school children graduated from high school at a rate more than a hundred times that for Irish or Italian children. Similar results were found in various other cities around the country.

Mental test scores, which are now supposed to be "racially biased," showed disparities among various groups of white children that were as great as those between blacks and whites today. Some of the low-I.Q. ethnic groups of the past now have average or even above-average I.Q.'s, so these scores are not fixed in concrete. But neither are they purely a matter of discrimination.

There must be some better way to advance disadvantaged groups than by tearing the country apart over wholly unsubstantiated theories about statistical "representation" in schools, jobs, and other activities. Polls show minorities themselves reject such theories.

9

A Look at History

LOS ANGELES HERALD EXAMINER / JANUARY 30, 1980

In the current controversy over such things as "white flight" and "affirmative action," we often see ourselves and our times as more special than they really are. Skin color differences also make it easy to see certain patterns between blacks and whites. But similar patterns have existed among people you could not tell apart with the naked eye.

When the Irish immigrants first arrived in America in the nineteenth century, old Anglo-Saxon families left their neighborhoods in great haste at the sign of the first Irishman moving in. Old German families moved out in a panic when the first Jewish immigrants moved in.

There were a few middle-class black families in northern cities during the great immigration era back around the turn of the century. They behaved just like the white middle class. When Polish immigrants started moving into their neighborhoods in Detroit, the blacks moved out. "Black flight" also occurred in New York, when Italian immigrants moved in. Harlem was once a middle-class white community. Middle-class blacks started moving in to get away from the Irish in midtown Manhattan.

Even busing controversies are not new. Back in 1904, the New York City Board of Education wanted to bus children from overcrowded schools on the East Side to West Side schools that had plenty of space. The only problem was that the East Side children were Jewish and the West Side children were Irish. The uproar was tremendous—and the Board of Education had to back down. The East Side schools just remained overcrowded.

The fact that something has been going on a long time doesn't mean that it is right. But it does undermine some of the popular theories about what is happening today. For example, it is often regarded as strange (or even sinister) when schoolchildren of one ethnic background are taught predominantly by teachers from a different background. Or when the rank and file of an organization are from one group and the leaders are from another. Or when people are not evenly "represented" in various activities according to their proportion of the population.

When the Irish immigrants' children went to public school, they were taught by Anglo-Saxon schoolteachers. There were very few educationally "qualified" Irish at that point. Similarly, when the Jewish immigrants' children went to school, decades later, their teachers were more

10

likely to be Irish than Jewish. Still later, when I went to school in Harlem a generation ago, most of my teachers were Jewish.

Similar patterns existed in politics and labor unions. Those who were there first and had more experience were likely to be leading those who came after them. Irish politicians represented Italian and Jewish neighborhoods on into the early twentieth century. Irish labor leaders likewise led unions long after the Irish rank and file had gone on to better things, replaced by new workers starting at the bottom. Elderly Jewish leaders heading predominantly black and Puerto Rican unions in New York today are nothing new.

For similar reasons, current programs for "minorities" in general are more than likely to fall under the control of blacks, who have been at this sort of thing longer. But most minority people in the country are not black.

Within the black community itself, there has been no random pattern of leadership "representation." Most top black leaders in history have come from families who somehow got a head start over other blacks in earlier generations. Some of their ancestors were freed from slavery long before the Civil War and were on their way up while other blacks were still in bondage.

W. E. B. DuBois and other founders and early leaders of the National Association for the Advancement of Colored People (NAACP) were from this background. So too is Supreme Court Justice Thurgood Marshall. Secretary of the Army Clifford Alexander and former U.N. Ambassador Andrew Young are from families that have gone to college for generations—that is, longer than most white Americans.

The overwhelming bulk of black professionals in this country come from a very few families, who typically have more than one doctor, lawyer, or academic. The alumni of five black high schools would account for almost all the leading black pioneers in medicine, law, the military, politics, and academia. There has been nothing random about it.

The American ideal is for each individual to stand or fall on his own individual performance, not the accident of birth. It just so happens that the accident of birth and upbringing turns out to have a profound effect on performance, or even on what the individual wants to do. No sinister Machiavelli planned it that way or pulled strings behind the scenes. Most whites in power have known little and cared less about the internal patterns of the black community.

There have been many deliberate actions and policies toward many groups that have needed correction—and still need correction. But claiming that every deviation from random statistical representation falls into that category is a very big and arbitrary assumption.

11

Black "Leaders" I

THE NEW YORK TIMES / APRIL 12, 1979

There is still some truth in the old cliché that blacks "all look alike" to whites. But enormous diversities within the black community are not only important in themselves; they also throw much-needed light on prevailing assumptions about the role of race in America.

Many black leaders, or "spokesmen," are from backgrounds highly atypical of the black population as a whole. Some are descended from families that were free long before the Civil War. The descendants of the antebellum "free persons of color" have continued to be disproportionately represented among prominent blacks well into the twentieth century. These include W. E. B. DuBois and virtually the whole generation of blacks among the founders of the NAACP, as well as such contemporary figures as Thurgood Marshall.

Another large, atypical source of black leadership has been West Indian immigrants and their descendants. These have included Malcolm X, Stokely Carmichael, Shirley Chisholm, Kenneth Clark, James Farmer, Roy Innes and virtually all the black borough presidents of Manhattan for a quarter of a century.

A leadership so atypical of the people for whom it claims to speak has many special problems that affect the leaders' priorities and strategies and the course of race relations in general. It is not only among the elite that internal differences among blacks are manifested. As of the 1970 census, the average family income of black West Indians in the United States was 44 percent higher than that among blacks as a whole. The proportion of West Indians in the professions was exactly double that of blacks in general, and the West Indians' unemployment rate was *below* the national average.

The social differences are as dramatic as the economic differences. Fertility rates among blacks are higher than among whites, but West Indians' fertility rate are below the national average—and even below a level required to reproduce themselves. When the sociologist Ira Reid studied West Indian crime rates in the 1930s, he found them lower than either black or white crime rates. (There has been no major study of West Indians in the last 40 years.)

Data on the pre-Civil War "free persons of color" and their descendants are harder to come by, but what is available also suggests sharp contrasts with the bulk of black Americans. By 1850, the "free persons of color" had achieved a level of literacy not reached by the black population as a whole until the beginning of the twentieth century; by 1860, the "free persons of color" had become urbanized to an extent not reached by blacks in general until about 1940.

The head start of this segment of the black community has had enduring consequences. Biographical studies of black doctoral degree holders in 1950 strongly suggest that most were descendants of "free persons of color." So do family data from a study of black professionals in Washington, D.C., in 1950. It is also well documented that the highest achieving black high school in American history was founded by "free persons of color" in nineteenth-century Washington. Over an 85-year period, that institution, Dunbar High School, sent most of its graduates on to college, at a time when most whites did not go on to college. The average I.Q. of its student body was above the national average in the 1930s. Its alumni included the first black general, the first black cabinet member, the first black federal judge, the first black senator elected in this century, and the discoverer of blood plasma.

West Indians and descendants of the old black elite have differed from most blacks not only by achievement but socially as well. For most of their history, both groups have ostracized most other blacks from their social circles. A study of West Indian women attending black American colleges in the 1930s found that 98 percent married West Indian men. A 1972 study of Barbadians in Brooklyn found that 87 percent married other Barbadians. Scattered studies have found comparable separation between the descendants of the old black elite and the masses of the black population, who lived in communities almost hermetically sealed from each other.

These differences among blacks and the atypical origins of black leaders carry broad implications. The values and priorities of the black population not only differ from those of the leadership but can even point in opposite directions.

Black "Leaders" II

THE NEW YORK TIMES / APRIL 13, 1979

Black leadership has come disproportionately from two highly atypical groups—descendants of blacks free before the Civil War and West Indian immigrants. Thus, much of the black leadership speaks in the name of a black population from which it differs socially and economically—and a population long despised by the groups in which the leaders have their own roots.

For a long time, the predominance of light-skinned Negroes in the black elite led many (including some in the elite) to credit white ancestry with their superior achievements. The proportion of mulattoes among the antebellum "free persons of color" was several times higher than among the slaves. But the later elite of West Indian origin has an even higher proportion of African ancestry than the American Negro population in general. So much for genetics.

Although white racism is often cited as a virtually complete explanation of black-white socio-economic differences, it can hardly explain the underrepresentation of blacks in the professions, for example, if black West Indians are *over*represented in the professions. The two kinds of blacks "all look alike" to racists, and even to many who are not racists. Similarly, if racism is the "root cause" of ghetto crime, why does this root sprout in one group but not the other?

Some people have claimed that West Indians are sorted out by whites and treated differently and that this explains the different economic results. This theory can be tested by looking at second-generation West Indians, who would be harder to sort out by such signs as accent, birthplace, or schools attended. Second-generation West Indians have even higher incomes than first-generation West Indians—and higher incomes than the U.S. national average.

The conclusion that color does not explain nearly as much as generally supposed is supported by recent studies. Richard Freeman, a Harvard economist, found that young adult blacks and whites with the same education and from homes with similar reading habits had the same incomes. That was not always true, but it had become so by the late 1960s. This is no consolation as far as the large income gap between blacks and whites is concerned, but it does suggest that some efforts directed toward employers might bring better results if directed toward schools or the home.

14

Reorienting the thinking of an individual or an organization is difficult under the best of circumstances. It is especially difficult for leaders with different social origins from the led. Such leaders often become "blacker than thou" as their own compensation for the past.

Not only guilt but also expediency promotes a more extreme political position among black leaders than among most of the black population. Polls show that most blacks oppose busing and affirmative action and are critical of the law for being too lenient with criminals. But black leaders, spokesmen, and organizations are spearheading drives in the opposite direction to these views. Black leaders share a social vision common among the white elite liberals with whom their lives are intertwined and from whom they receive the favorable publicity and financial support essential to their role as black leaders.

In many cases, their very "leadership" consists not of their having been selected by blacks but of being regarded by the white news media, white philanthropy, and white politicians as "spokesmen" for the black masses. Much of the black leadership is not in the business of leading blacks but of extracting what they can from whites, and their strategies and rhetoric reflect that orientation.

The historical enormity of slavery and the modern problem of discrimination are invoked to explain everything from black families' being headed by women to crime rates in Harlem, high unemployment among black teenagers, and the degeneration of ghetto schools into blackboard jungles. The fervor behind such assertions is not based on evidence but rather is used to preclude examination of evidence.

In reality, black families have been predominantly two-parent families headed by males, under both slavery and freedom, until recent decades. The black family held together during centuries of slavery and generations of oppression. The large and growing numbers of one-parent, female-headed families have emerged in recent decades, as the welfare system has subsidized both male desertion and teenage pregnancy.

If racism and discrimination are the explanations of high black teenage unemployment, why were their unemployment rates only one-fifth as high in the early 1950s as in the 1970s? Was there less racism and discrimination then? Economists all over the country have been turning out studies showing that the unemployment of black teenagers has been caused by escalating minimum-wage laws—which are still being pushed by the black "leadership."

Neither the runaway crime rates in general nor school violence in particular were comparable in the lean and segregated 1930s to what has been seen in the 1970s. Harlem was a place where people could sleep

15

out on fire escapes, tenement roofs, and even in parks on hot summer nights in the 1930s. In school, neither principals, parents, nor the criminal justice system tolerated the kind of outrages that have since become common.

A black "leadership" attuned to the susceptibilities of white liberals may invoke historical explanations that do not stand up under factual scrutiny. A black leadership more attuned to its own people might ask what has so undermined the black family and the black community within the past generation, and whether it has anything to do with the kinds of policies that that leadership has advocated and still advocates.

Blacks and I.Q. Tests

LOS ANGELES HERALD EXAMINER / OCTOBER 3, 1979

Professor Arthur R. Jensen at Berkeley has once more burst forth into the media with his now familiar claim that racial differences in I.Q. are hereditary. The new studies are based on physical reaction times, which Jensen says differ between blacks and whites. It is too early for Jensen's new findings to be taken apart and carefully studied by specialists, as they surely will be in time. But anyone who watches basketball will require a lot of convincing that blacks' reactions are slower than whites'. In baseball, where the ball goes from the pitcher's hand to the catcher's mitt in less than a second, blacks have higher batting averages than whites.

Jensen's new approach would be more credible if he had paused to deal with evidence that undermined his old approach, which dealt with I.Q. statistics. Perhaps the most devastating evidence against him was a recent study of black orphans raised by white families. These youngsters had higher I.Q.'s than the national average. Their heredity was the same as that of other black youngsters, but their environment was obviously very different. Jensen has simply ignored that study and gone on to something else.

Historical statistics on I.Q.'s also undermine Jensen's claim. Back around World War I, Americans of Italian, Polish, and Jewish ancestry had mental test scores very much like those of blacks today. However, as those groups rose economically and socially, their I.Q.'s also rose dramatically and now equal or exceed the national average. Despite the popularity of so-called Polish jokes, the average I.Q. of Polish-Americans today is above the national average, though fifty years ago it was the same as blacks'. Jensen has also never confronted this evidence.

Perhaps more important than Jensen's theories or the evidence for or against them is the social impact of the controversy that has swirled around him for ten years now. The powerful emotions generated on all sides has prevented even Jensen's own position from being accurately reported in the media and has led others to blind, vehement attacks on mental tests themselves, much like the old practice of killing the messenger that brought bad news.

Jensen himself did not use his original study of ten years ago to argue that black youngsters could not learn in school. On the contrary, he concluded that they could be taught the same material much more

17

effectively by using different teaching methods. This point almost never came out in the sensationalized press accounts of the controversy.

The great tragedy is that the outrage aroused by Jensen's theories has led to the banning of I.Q. tests in New York and other cities and to paranoid attacks on all kinds of tests or other intellectual standards for jobs, college admissions, or admission to the practice of law. But the problem is not that the tests were unfair. The problem is that life is unfair, and the tests are measuring the consequences.

As a child moving from an all-black school in the South to an all-black school in Harlem, I suddenly found myself changed from the top student in my class to the bottom student. The problem was not that the tests were biased. The problem was that my previous education was grossly inadequate. Throwing out the tests would have done no more good than breaking a thermometer when it showed that I had a fever. It was not "fair" that I suddenly found myself trailing behind all my classmates. But it would have been even more unfair—and permanently crippling—to have kept me unaware of how much work I had to make up.

To take away testing in the school system would hurt black youngsters worse than it would hurt whites. Educated middle-class parents can tell whether the schools are doing a good job or not, and they carry enough political weight to keep the schools from completely neglecting their children's education. Fewer black parents have had the benefit of the kind of education or the kind of political clout that would enable them to keep the schools from shortchanging their children. Test scores at least provide some evidence of what is going on, and even the smallest help in monitoring the school's performance should not be thrown away.

Test scores have been superstitiously worshipped for too long. The answer, however, is not an equally irrational refusal to get whatever small help they can provide. I.Q. tests have their limitations, like everything human. But, used with this in mind, they can be one of many tools to cope with problems and opportunities.

As for the broader issues of race as an explanation of economic and other success, the complexities go well beyond any of the simple answers in any part of the spectrum. Black West Indians in the United States have incomes very similar to other Americans—and a higher proportion of African ancestry than American blacks. Second-generation West Indians in the United States have higher incomes than Anglo-Saxons. Obviously, there is much more involved than either race or racism.

18

The Resignation of Andrew Young

LOS ANGELES HERALD EXAMINER / AUGUST 22, 1979

With the impending passing of U.N. Ambassador Andrew Young from the national political scene—not a moment too soon—perhaps we should just be happy that we will not have to hear his big mouth again or see his foot in it. But there is a deeper tragedy here that goes beyond this one glib and shallow man.

Young is going out in character—not a bit sorry that he has thrown a monkey wrench into some of the most delicate and important peace negotiations of this generation. If those negotiations fail, your son or mine may someday have to go shed his blood in some Middle East desert and perhaps be buried there. But that seems less important to Ambassador Young than preserving his macho image as unbowed and defiant—standing up to The Man. If he wants to engage in psychodrama as a private citizen, he has every right to do so under the First Amendment. But that is very different from carrying on his own separate, personal foreign policy while being paid as an official of the U.S. government.

Like many people who do a lot of posturing as champions of the oppressed, Young himself was from a privileged background. Generations of his family had gone to college before him, unlike most Americans of any color. No doubt the color of his skin kept Andy Young from enjoying all of the privileges that his affluence would otherwise have brought. But his problems were not the problems of the poor, and his radical chic outlook on the world today is very different from that of working-class black people. Polls have repeatedly shown most black Americans rejecting preferential treatment (quotas), busing, or leniency toward criminals. That kind of hogwash is for the sheltered elite of both races—the Andrew Youngs of whatever color.

Young's old cronies in the civil rights movement may try to create the impression that masses of blacks are going to rise up in righteous wrath at the ambassador's departure, threatening whites in general and Jews in particular. It is not only a despicable tactic but a ridiculous hoax. It is doubtful if anybody in Harlem is worked up enough to even stop buying Levy's rye bread.

Young and his apologists have often reminded us that he speaks from the perspective of a former civil rights leader. How much of a civil rights leader Andrew Young was is open to question, but at least he hung

19

around people who were leaders. The real question is, to what extent did that broaden his perspective, and to what extent did it narrow his vision?

The civil rights movement—and, indeed, the whole history of blacks in this country—can be seen as part of the great tapestry of human history and of the struggle for freedom. There were whites in the civil rights movement who marched and were jailed and killed because they saw it as part of a broader human struggle. That struggle has had many landmarks, from Gettysburg to the Gulag Archipelago. *Roots* has been translated into the language of people of every color on every continent, because ultimately it is the story of the human spirit.

Narrower people have looked at the civil rights movement in a more petty way. To the narrow-minded of both races, it was little more than a drive to "get whitey" or an opportunity to promote a hustle or to get media coverage. Andrew Young often seemed to draw little more from his civil rights experience than perpetual one-upmanship against whites.

Even the fate of blacks, in America and around the world, was viewed in this petty framework. The sickening atrocities of Idi Amin against masses of Africans never aroused the angry rhetoric that Young unleashed against white governments he disagreed with, or even against the new black government in Rhodesia that isn't far enough left for his taste. The tens of thousands of people put to agonizing, sadistic deaths in the African nation of Guinea likewise never seemed to stir his oratory.

Why this unusual reticence in the face of mass atrocities, and vehement outbursts against political policies? It suggests that Young is more concerned with protecting the *image* of blacks—which is to say, his own standing among whites—than with the actual fate of flesh-and-blood black people.

Government by Snobs

LOS ANGELES HERALD EXAMINER / JUNE 6, 1979

The recall of Howard Miller from the Los Angeles School Board may help other public officials to recall who put them in office. It is also worthwhile to recall how we got into the hideous mess that goes by the label of busing.

Ironically, it all began 25 years ago because the parents of a little girl named Linda Brown did not want her to be bused to a distant school when there was a public school much nearer where she lived. But the politicians and bureaucrats had decided that they would assign children to schools according to their race. Sometimes, the more things change, the more they remain the same.

Virtually every segment of the population—by race, region, or class—is opposed to forced busing. Why does it continue, then? Because a relative handful of the anointed have decided that they know what is "really" good for us. Like the politicians, bureaucrats, and judges who once maintained forced segregation in the public schools, they do not hesitate to use children as guinea pigs for an ideology. Forced segregation was an uglier ideology, but forcing people apart and forcing them together have both had disastrous consequences. Neither has any place in a democracy.

The legal revolution that began with *Brown* vs. *Board of Education* in 1954 has become more and more plainly an antidemocratic trend. At first this was overlooked, because the Supreme Court was striking down painful discriminatory policies that were already beginning to crumble, as public opinion became more enlightened.

Segregation in public places in Washington, D.C. ended by voluntary agreement two years before the Supreme Court decision, and was starting to erode in the border states and to be questioned even in the Deep South. Desegregation was an idea whose time had come. How, and through which mechanisms, did not seem to matter at the time. Now we know that this decision was only the first step toward an unprecedented expansion of the power of judges that went way beyond questions of race.

Because the courts began by attacking policies that were repugnant to increasing numbers of thoughtful people, questions or criticisms were dismissed as quibbles, and critics were branded as racists or reactionaries. If all else failed, the ponderous phrase "the law of the land" could be invoked. It meant not only that we should obey court orders, but that

21

we should shut up after a judge had expressed an opinion.

But as the passing years brought more and more freewheeling judicial policymaking in fields from crime to contraception, even some of the early supporters of judicial activism began to speak up in opposition. The most illustrious example was the late Professor Alexander Bickel of the Yale Law School. Originally a staunch defender of the Warren court, for whom he had been a clerk, Bickel abandoned his earlier conviction that the judiciary was "the least dangerous branch" of government and began to write about the immorality of having appointed judges attempting to govern without the consent of the governed.

Against this background, Howard Miller and the pious hokum that surrounded him can be seen as a local attempt to maintain the old cant and govern against the consent of the governed. People who elected Miller to use the legal processes available to oppose and appeal busing orders were rightly angered that he (1) failed to do so, (2) piously claimed to be only "obeying the law" when in fact he was abandoning legal redress, and (3) became part of the cover-up of the disastrous consequences of busing by witholding meaningful statistics on student withdrawals.

The anointed elite, in newspaper and television editorials, joined Miller in this shameful equating of law-abiding behavior with abandon-ment of the legal redress provided by the Constitution itself. The repudi-ation of Miller was also a repudiation of the Establishment's we-know-best deception in favor of more fundamental principles of representative government. As long as the majority of people is ready to think for itself, in opposition to the virtually unanimous chorus of the self-anointed "moral leaders," the battle for democracy is not yet lost.

No doubt Miller will be depicted as some sort of martyr to some sort of cause. He is, in fact, a man who lied to get his job and lied to keep it. More important, what he represented was the denial of the democratic process in favor of the vogues of the self-righteous few. We are well rid of him.

We will be well rid of any others who think that the public's role is to shut up and do whatever some judge wants them to. Eventually, we may also want to rewrite the laws that give one headstrong judge the power to wreak such havoc in the lives of thousands of children who have committed no crime.

Bakke and the Backlash

THE WASHINGTON STAR / JULY 8, 1978

Amid all the controversies surrounding the Bakke case, there is one significant but little-noticed fact on which both sides agreed. Both Bakke and the Davis Medical School admitted early in the case that they could not sustain the burden of proof as to whether or not he would have been admitted even if there were no minority admissions program at all. There were enough other whites better qualified, and the admissions procedure was sufficiently complex, that no one will ever know whether any minority medical student ever cost Bakke anything.

This in no way denigrates the resolve and courage of Bakke or the historic significance of his case. But it is a clue to what has been most dangerous about the whole "affirmative action" approach. The resentment and bitterness that have been built up by quotas and preferences extend far beyond those who have in fact lost anything.

Indeed, recent studies indicate that blacks gained little or nothing overall from affirmative action. Black income as a percentage of white income reached its peak in 1970—the year before "goals and time-tables"—and has never been that high again since. Even some of the strongest supporters of "affirmative action" have bitterly complained that it isn't really working. Why then the enormous backlash against it?

First of all, the principle of quotas is galling. The use of race is galling. The whole civil rights movement was based ultimately on that simple fact, even though many civil rights leaders now find it hard to understand why others are angry at what made them angry. They insist that the situation of blacks is different. And they are right. Everyone's situation is different.

But what makes any kind of human society possible is that there are certain basic similarities despite all differences, including similarities on things that make us mad. Indeed, the principles behind quotas are so offensive to Americans that most blacks, most women, and every regional, educational, or income group studied by the Gallup poll were opposed to preferential treatment in hiring or college admission. Backlash against quotas is as American as apple pie—or soul food.

The manner in which quotas were imposed was almost as much resented as the quotas themselves. The arrogance of the bureaucrats administering quotas is a story unto itself. The overlapping jurisdictions of the agencies involved, their conflicting interpretations, and the

23

liability to lawsuits for "reverse discrimination" (even if all the government agencies sanctioned a particular affirmative action program) made this an embattled legal no-man's-land.

Law is supposed to tell you in advance what you can and cannot do, not simply strike you like lightning from the blue after you have done it. But affirmative action has been a question of steering a twisting course through the rocks of various administrative agencies, minority and female individuals ready to claim "discrimination," and white males ready to claim "reverse discrimination." It was not a law but a mine field.

Where does the Supreme Court decision leave us? Although various opposing groups are all claiming "victory," as they do in presidential primaries, a five-to-four decision on a matter of fundamental constitutional rights cannot be wholly satisfactory to anyone. Such a close decision means that the trumpet has made an uncertain sound. Moreover, a change in the health of just one of these nine gentlemen could change the history of this nation.

However, the carefully reasoned decision of Mr. Justice Powell gives some hope that the Supreme Court has recognized not only the problems of quotas but also the limits of its own ability to redress every historic grievance. Still frightening, however, is Justice Blackmun's dissenting opinion approving "transitional inequality," for which there is no authorization either in the Constitution or in statutory law. The idea that the Supreme Court can just "wing it" with its own policymaking is still not dead. And the proposition that they continue to wing it until such indefinite time as the undefined "transition" is over is even more staggering.

The Supreme Court majority has drawn a line and said that certain practices—quotas by whatever name—are simply "out." What that will mean in practice remains for history to unfold. Still, it is a principled and important landmark in a troubled area.

What neither the majority nor the dissenters squarely faced is the meaning of "equality"—whether it is prospective equality of opportunity or retrospective equality of statistical results. Hovering in the background of the dissenting opinions is a social vision that would equate the two, that would say implicitly that random results are inevitable without societal bias in decisionmaking.

This easy assumption waves aside the whole thrust of each group's own culture or even such basic demographic facts of life as age differences between different ethnic groups, which can range up to a decade or even a quarter of a century, depending upon the groups. Nowhere in life do we find this random distribution of people, even in activities wholly within our own individual control, such as our choice of card games, television programs, or child-rearing practices. We are not random numbers, and this decision says that we cannot be treated as if we were.

There is much that remains to be done by and for disadvantaged minorities. Now that an illusory shortcut has been blocked, perhaps we can turn our attention to more progress on the main road.

2

POLITICS

THESE ARE ESSAYS ABOUT politics in the broad sense—not Democrats versus Republicans, or this personality against that. They are about how a political system works—or doesn't work. They deal with how we see ourselves politically and the assumptions on which we act. The topics covered vary from bureaucracy to terrorism, but the underlying concern is about our vision of the world. How much of what we believe will stand up under scrutiny? How much is fact, how much illusion? How much does the prevailing political vision meet our emotional needs of the moment rather than face the enduring realities confronting our generation and generations to come?

Realism is too often the missing ingredient in American politics. In its place are moral passion and ringing rhetoric. Some are still looking for a political messiah who will lead us into the promised land. Others, who consider themselves more sophisticated, are looking for "experts" who can "solve" our problems, as if they were academic exercises in a text-book. Both the messiah and the expert are projections of our desperate attempt to turn our difficulties and responsibilities over to someone else. Unfortunately, there are also many people ready to assume the role of messiah or expert for the power it will give them. Cold facts lend no more support to the claims of experts than to the claims of messiahs. But experts are newer, more modern, and they use language that is more "scientific" in its mystification. The actual results of their efforts have been a series of disasters, ranging from education to crime to the economy. The purpose of these essays is not simply to point out these disasters, but to suggest some of the political attitudes and assumptions that threaten similar disasters if the same way of thinking continues.

Who Says
Bureaucracy Is Inefficient?

THE WASHINGTON STAR / NOVEMBER 1, 1977

Wouldn't it seem strange if A were always accusing B of stupidity and inefficiency while B's income was higher than A's, B's income was growing faster than A's, and B's power over A was constantly increasing? This is precisely the situation as regards the public (A), which criticizes government bureaucrats (B). The public has all too many reasons to be unhappy and angry with bureaucrats. But to blame problems in Washington on stupidity and inefficiency among government officials is to misunderstand what is happening.

Government employees are better paid than private employees, have lower unemployment rates, and fatter pensions. As for their workload, when was the last time you saw a civil servant perspiring on the job (President Nixon doesn't count)? The highest income county in the United States is in a suburb of Washington. Recent polls show personal optimism about the future higher in the Washington area than in the country at large—and that optimism is well placed, as regards their own future. Bureaucracy is a growth industry. This has been true over the years regardless of which party was in power and regardless of whether the particular president was called liberal, conservative, or a born-again Christian out to reform "the mess in Washington."

Conservatives used to have the inside track on criticizing high-living Washington functionaries who mouthed egalitarian platitudes over caviar and filet mignon. Now the plush Washington lifestyle has become a scandal to liberals as well. The *New Republic* recently devoted a whole issue to exposing the luxurious life-style of Washington bureaucrats, their expense-account living, and the double standard that permits them to prescribe quotas and busing for the rest of the country while sending their own children to one of the most segregated school systems in the country.

The bureaucracy, with its financial security and special privileges, is, if anything, far too smart and too efficient in promoting its own interest. The rest of us would do well to get smart and understand how it happened. In order to know if people are "efficient" or "inefficient," you have to know what they are trying to do. Fan dancing is a very inefficient way of circulating the air in a room, but it is a very efficient way of transferring money from the pockets of the viewers to the pocket of the performer. The government is not fan dancing, but there is a similar emphasis on going through tantalizing motions that promise more than is delivered.

The crucial mistake is to assume that the government's purpose is our purpose. We may see something "wrong" in the world and imagine that it follows, as the night follows the day, that "there ought to be a law"— and a program and an agency to carry out the law, to protect us from whatever evil is in vogue at the moment. Now, things have been going wrong ever since we got off on the wrong foot in the garden of Eden, but hope springs eternal that some new collection of bureaucrats will put a stop to it. This hope is the inexhaustible raw material from which bureaucratic empires are built.

Efficiency means getting the most output with the least input. But bureaucrats are paid according to how many other bureaucrats work under them and how big a budget they administer. This is called being paid for the level of responsibility. Obviously, the more people hired and the more money spent to get a given job done, the higher the level of responsibility and therefore the higher the salary. To call overstaffing and unnecessary paperwork "inefficiency" or stupidity in this context is to miss the whole point.

What we may call bureaucratic delay is someone else's job protection and his boss's salary justification. The same people can move tremendous numbers of pieces of paper with great speed, as they do in government agencies where thousands of numbers-racket bets are collected, coordinated, and paid off every day.

Bungling? When was the last time government workers missed getting their paychecks, in full and on time? Confusion? When was the last time government workers' unions failed to torpedo reforms that would cost jobs? Few things have been as much criticized as the welfare system and the education system, and yet the only reforms that have any political chance in these areas must first and foremost assure the jobs, power, and appropriations of the existing bureaucrats.

Efficient? Very.

A Christmas Parable

LOS ANGELES HERALD EXAMINER / DECEMBER 25, 1979

"Sir, I am an investigator for the federal government. Here are my credentials. I'd like to ask you some questions."

"All right."

"First, I understand that you built a rather large project some time ago."

"Yes."

"What was the nature of that project?"

"Creating the heavens and the earth."

"That sounds like a sizable undertaking. Did you have a permit from the zoning board and the coastal commission?"

"No."

"Had you filed an environmental impact report?"

"No."

"Were your production facilities inspected by the Occupational Safety and Health Administration?"

"No."

"This doesn't look good. How did your project begin?"

"I said, 'Let there be light.' "

"Light? Let me write that down in my report."

"It has already been written down, many years ago."

"But I still need this for my files. Where did you get the light?"

"Where?"

"Yes. Was it from a nuclear plant?"

"No."

"Good. Their safety is still under investigation. Did you use fossil fuels?"

"No."

"Good. There are many regulatory provisions to which you would be subject."

"Perhaps not."

"Well, I won't argue the legal technicalities with you. Our attorneys will be contacting you on that. Let me ask you another question. What was the express purpose and operating procedure of your project?"

"It was for people."

"People? Both male and female?"

"Yes."

31

"Black? White? Oriental?"

"Everyone."

"Did you file a report showing that they would be proportionally represented in each specific activity of your project, as required by the Equal Employment Opportunity Commission?"

"No."

"Were there any children?"

"Yes. The people were to multiply and replenish the earth."

"Did you, at that time, check the census population figures?"

"No."

"Had you read about overpopulation projections, the zero-growth literature, or the 'small is beau_ _ul' philosophy?"

"No."

"Quite frankly, sir, you don_   _l informed. Do you have a college degree?"

"No."

"I thought not. Still, igr   use. Let me ask you some personal questions   you live?"

"Everywhere."

"I'm afraid I'll have   rt: a transient with no fixed address. It is m_   at could be used against you in a court of la_

"A court of law? 1 h_   igated or accused before."

"Well, the federal jurisu_   vity are increasing all the time."

"Perhaps too much."

"The courts will decide that, sir. That's what we have courts for. Let me ask you another question: Do you have any children?"

"A son."

"When was he born?"

"On the twenty-fifth of this month."

"Well, if you are planning a birthday celebration, you may go ahead without fear of being embarrassed by more of our investigators showing up that day. It happens to be a holiday."

"I know."

"Equal Rights"
or Indiscriminate Treatment?

THE WASHINGTON STAR / MAY 2, 1978

If a woman has as much right to apply for a job as guard in a women's prison as a man has to apply for a job as guard in a man's prison, that is equal rights. But if men and women are assigned to work as prison guards without regard to the sex of the prisoners, that is *indiscriminate* treatment. It is also stupidity.

Much of the opposition to the Equal Rights Amendment (ERA) is based on the prospect of indiscriminant treatment mindlessly applied as "the law of the land." People who might find nothing objectionable in the literal words of the proposed amendment know all too well from recent experience how easily "equal rights" can be perverted to mean indiscriminant results. Crusaders for ERA are in fact constantly pointing to existing statistical results that they don't like, which will presumably be changed by ERA. We don't need to constitutionalize numbers games.

Despite many numbers that are thrown around, supposedly showing the "underrepresentation" or "underpayment" of women, most of the economic differences between men and women turn out, in fact, to be differences between married women and all other persons.

Single women in their thirties who have worked continuously since high school earn slightly more than single men in their thirties who have worked continuously since high school. And this was true even before "affirmative action." Single academic women with Ph.D.'s become full professors to a greater extent than males who received their Ph.D.'s at the same time. This too has been true for years.

Married women don't do nearly as well in most occupations for reasons that are obvious to anyone familiar with the responsibilities of wives and mothers. Married men do better in their careers than single men or single women for reasons that are equally obvious to anyone familiar with how much of their personal and social needs and responsibilities are taken care of by their wives.

For the same reason that a married woman can put less time into her career than a single woman, a married man can put more time into his career than a single man, relying on his wife to take care of everything from sex to socks. Whatever the merits or demerits of the present division of domestic responsibilities, it is not employer discrimination on the job.

Full-time single workers who are making it on their own earn about

33

the same, regardless of whether they are male or female.

The statistics thrown around by various women's spokesmen lump together the highly differing incomes of single and married women (many of the latter being part-timers) or include widows and divorcees in their definition of "single" women. Obviously, a woman in her thirties or forties who has been a housewife for a decade or two cannot reenter the labor market, after her husband is gone, at the same level as a man who has been working full time all the years she was taking care of a home and children.

But telling the plain truth about obvious realities would destroy the bulk of the arguments used to generate outrage and political pressure for indiscriminant results disguised as "equal rights." The economic vulnerability of the many women who invest in their husbands' careers instead of their own is one reason for alimony and other special legal treatment of women, all of which could be jeopardized by indiscriminant treatment of the sexes.

A look back through history makes it even more obvious how important domestic responsibilities have been in explaining women's careers. Despite propaganda claiming that recent political "struggles" have brought women "a long way," the cold fact is that women were far better "represented" in many high-level positions in decades or even generations past.

A higher percentage of doctors, academics, and people in the professions generally were women forty or fifty years ago. The reason was simply that a smaller proportion of educated women married then, and they did not have children as soon or as often. As the age of marriage declined and the number of children rose, the proportion of women in high-level positions declined. It had nothing to do with "male chauvinism."

Women certainly deserve equal rights. Few people of either sex would deny that, and, in fact, polls show men's opinions to be virtually identical with women's on issues revolving around the legal status of women. In fact, a slightly higher percentage of men than women favor ERA.

There is no great struggle between the sexes going on. There is a crusade led by so-called liberated women, promoting their special interests as the interests of all women, and a counterattempt by other women to hold on to protections made necessary by the way men and women differ physically, in life patterns, and in the division of domestic responsibilities.

"Expert" Failures

LOS ANGELES HERALD EXAMINER / DECEMBER 5, 1979

Have you noticed how many disasters follow in the wake of "experts"? The period since World War II has been the great era of experts on raising children. Dr. Spock was only the tip of the iceberg. You couldn't turn on the radio or television, or open a newspaper or magazine, without encountering an army of experts on how to raise your kid.

The first thing these experts emphasized was that laymen were all wrong in their approach. What we needed was the sophisticated, modern way to handle children, not simplistic or traditional methods. What followed was an unprecedented rise in juvenile delinquency, crime, teenage suicide, venereal disease, and pregnancy. The only thing going down was performance in school.

Experts on crime have come into their own in the same postwar era. Their first order of business has also been to argue that laymen don't understand. Here again, simplistic, traditional notions had to give way to modern sophistication. Murder rates had been declining for about twenty years under our misguided and simplistic beliefs. They tripled in less than a decade after the sophisticated expertise was put into practice by the courts in the 1960s. The pattern with other crimes of violence was very much the same.

Prison wardens used to be people with no special training. They were simply promoted from the ranks of guards or other prison personnel. They relied on their own experience rather than scientific expertise. As of the mid-1960s, for example, not one prison warden in California had a college degree. But by the mid-1970s, they were replaced by the new breed of prison wardens, most of whom had master's degrees. This was part of a national trend.

How did prisons run by sophisticated experts compare with prisons run the old-fashioned way? Murders among inmates more than tripled in a decade. Attacks on prison guards rose, as did their turnover rate. Inmate gangs gained more control of prison life on a day-to-day basis, as well as during the riots which became ever more frequent.

Experts took over control of the American money supply even earlier in history. A monetary crisis in the early twentieth century led to the creation of the Federal Reserve system in 1914. With experts in firm control of our money supply, we were supposed to have less sudden reductions in the flow of money, fewer bank failures, and less inflation.

In reality, however, the worst reduction in the flow of money ever seen in American history occurred under these experts. The amount of money in circulation dropped by one-third from 1929 to 1932. This made it impossible to buy as much, produce as much, employ as many people, or pay off mortgages on homes or farms. This disaster made all previous reductions in money supply look like child's play, and previous depressions look like minor incidents.

The largest number of bank failures ever seen also occurred under these experts: one-fourth of all the banks in the United States failed in one year. As for inflation, there has never been such a long period of inflation as we have had under the Federal Reserve system, especially in recent years.

While experts are quick to claim credit for anything good that happens, all disasters are attributed to something else. Those who believe in government economic activism attribute the Great Depression of the 1930s to business, or even to sinister plots by business to profit from other people's misery. Actually, profits declined faster than wages, and corporations as a whole operated billions of dollars in the red for two years in a row.

Earl Warren in his memoirs attributed the great amount of violent crime in America to "our disturbed society" or to poverty and the like. Yet this "disturbed" society had had declining murder rates for years before Warren led the crusade for a new theory of criminal law.

The many disasters striking American teenagers today are often blamed on parents. But before putting all the blame there, it is necessary to realize that the law and the schools have taken more and more decisions out of parents' hands.

The great problem with experts is that they don't know and can't know. They may have a lot of theories and second-hand information at their fingertips. But the hard, specific knowledge needed to make decisions is usually scattered among millions of laymen. The layman is the real expert on his own particular situation and has every incentive to change his decision when the results don't turn out the way he wants. The so-called expert tries to know too much from too far away and has no incentive to admit he is wrong, since someone else pays the price of his mistakes.

The great political problem is that we take experts too seriously. True, one expert may know more than one layman. But neither of them knows enough to try to control a whole economy or society of millions of other human beings. The layman at least realizes that his knowledge is inadequate to even attempt such a thing. The expert doesn't. That is why he is so dangerous.

The 1970s and 1980s

LOS ANGELES HERALD EXAMINER / DECEMBER 20, 1979

As we approach the end of this year, we are also approaching the end of a decade. It is hard to believe that the 1970s have come and gone. It seems like the 1960s were just here, with all the marching and slogans and great promises. The 1970s have left no such vivid images. That may be why this decade slipped away almost unnoticed.

Much of the political activity of the 1970s seemed to be merely trying to apply the great visions and programs of the 1960s—and watching them fail, one by one. "Innovative," unstructured, and gimmick-ridden education led to students who could not read or think. Trying to eliminate poverty only led to more dependency. Attempts to carry out a vision of a more racially harmonious society only led to increased animosities. Attempts to defuse international tensions only led to repeated setbacks and humiliations, and an increased vulnerability to a growing Soviet arsenal.

As the 1970s draw to a close, there are signs that many people have learned from these shattered visions. Proposition 13 shows that some of us have had it with giving the government our hard-earned money in exchange for glowing rhetoric and heady promises. Attempts to put some teeth back into criminal law show that people are no longer willing to be mugged or murdered as the price of someone else's social theories or "rehabilitation" experiments. The Senate's balking at the SALT II treaty shows that some people are no longer ready to jeopardize our security for the sake of international public relations, or to turn defense expenditures into domestic give-away programs.

The 1960s philosophy was basically that you could take what existed for granted and just tinker with it to make it better. That most of the world did not have the things we took for granted—our freedom, our prosperity, our stability of government—was just of-coursed aside. The name of the game was creating "solutions" to our "problems," as if life were an academic exercise with answers in the back of the book. There was little fear of playing with fire, even though we could see conflagrations raging in various countries around the world.

Ideals are necessary for any civilization. But, like many other things that are absolutely essential for life, an overdose can be fatal. We have to have salt, fats, and carbohydrates for physical survival, and yet most of us get so much of them that they shorten our lives. In the 1960s we overdosed on heady idealism, and much of the 1970s were our hang-over—millions on welfare in an economy with jobs going begging, skyrocketing crime rates among people better off than their ancestors had ever been, and anti-Americanism becoming an international sport among people living off the Yankee dollar.

While hangovers cause some people to want to give up the stuff, it causes others to want to escape with another high. Most Americans recognize the failure of the 1960s visions in the 1970s. But the true believers feel that those visions just weren't tried hard enough, long enough, or with enough tax money. They are still hoping for the second coming of Kennedy.

The 1970s were a decade when we had to discover some of the basic facts of life the hard way. The relentless necessities of civilization cannot be of-coursed aside. Nor can the people or institutions or traditions that meet those necessities be constantly undermined by those on a moral jag, without all of us suffering. The blessings of civilization that we take for granted require constant efforts and dedication, and occasionally desparate courage. Anytime we falter, barbarism is right there, ready to move in. If we need reminders of how close it is, we can see it in such things as the trampling of people to death at a recent rock concert, or we can read about the atrocities that abound in each day's news about despots abroad or criminals at home. We can sleep at night only because of others who do not sleep, but stand guard on even the most festive or sacred days.

The fight against barbarism is a fight that is never over. New barbarians are born into our midst every day, ignorant as the caveman and with all his destructive passions. And there are only a few brief years in which to civilize them. With some the job never gets done. We can no longer afford the 1960s romantic crusade against "inhibitions," because without inhibitions we are all barbarians.

The 1980s are an opportunity to go forward with a new maturity and sense of realism. We should not have to repeat the 1960s and 1970s again.

Political Perpetual Motion

LOS ANGELES HERALD EXAMINER / JULY 11, 1979

If there is anything more common than denunciations of government bureaucracies, it is the growth of government bureaucracies in spite of all denunciations.

The urban renewal program has been hit with devastating scholarly critiques, journalistic exposés, political attacks, and bitter street demonstrations—and its budget has tripled in less than a decade. The government's various farm programs have been under at least equally severe attack for a much longer period of time; but between 1950 and 1970, government payments to farmers increased tenfold, although the number of farmers was reduced by half. Likewise, expenditures on the public schools have risen exponentially, while the number of students has declined along with their reading and math scores.

Why do the critics of bureaucracy win the battles and lose the wars? Because they are simply outmanned and outgunned. A congressman and his staff can launch an attack on a bureaucracy and perhaps hold the press's attention for a few days, or a few weeks at most. But eventually the congressional office must spread itself thin over a hundred different issues while the bureaucracy can put ten times as many people to work countering that one attack. It can put hundreds more people to work year-round, forestalling attacks by the way they phrase their objectives to the public, maintain their relationships with important interest groups, award grants and consulting contracts to sympathetic "experts," produce special benefits in the districts of key congressmen, and insulate their performance from scrutiny with arcane jargon and by burying key facts in masses of irrelevant statistics.

Most government programs are evaluated by the very agencies that run them. Even "outside" evaluations are generally by "experts" chosen by the agency. Under these circumstances, it is hardly surprising to find in these evaluations a virtually unbroken record of "success," tempered only by the need for more money, more staff, and broader powers "in order to do an even better job in the future." Where problems or scandals have already come to light, they too will be corrected with more money, more staff, and broader powers. It is a heads-I-win-tails-you-lose situation.

The academic and "think tank" researchers who surround a bureaucracy are politically very important. They appear before Congress, the

39

media, and the public as impartial witnesses to the "need" for the programs from which they are personally receiving consulting fees and grants.

When other special interest groups testify before Congress, they are immediately identified by their affiliation and their statements discounted accordingly. But a professor who appears as a witness is identified only by his university affiliation, and no one asks if he has received thousands of dollars in consulting fees or hundreds of thousands in grants from the very agency whose program he is discussing.

He is received by congressional committees as an impartial expert, giving of his wisdom in the public interest. When he is quoted in newspapers, it is billed as news, not advertising. When he appears on television talk shows to urge the need for this, or the dire consequences of a budget cut in that, he neither pays the price of an advertiser nor bears the stigma of a commercial. Instead, he is thanked by the host for "taking the time out of your busy schedule" to come and "enlighten" the television audience "on this important subject."

Government agencies with vast research funds to award to universities and "think tanks" can field a battalion of "experts" on their programs to fight their battles on many fronts. Nor need all these consultants and grant recipients be simply "hired guns." It may well be that "for every Ph.D., there is an equal and opposite Ph.D.," but the government agency can choose to bankroll those sincerely sympathetic to its programs and boycott those known to be sincerely critical. The net result can be one side with more voluminous research behind its position, with the other side reduced to speaking in generalities or making methodological criticisms, neither of which is very effective.

Those experts who support a particular government program (or are sympathetic to government programs in general) have whole careers open to them, alternating as government officials, "think tank" researchers, and university professors; supplying consulting services, evaluation reports, and published writings in both scholarly journals and the mass media.

These revolving door careers—going in and out of government—mean numerous valuable connections with other like-minded experts. Those who are on the inside at any given time hand out grants and consulting contracts to their compatriots on the outside, and as time goes on, they change places, the former recipients now becoming donors of government money to their former benefactors.

In some areas, such as development economics, the very existence of the field itself is largely dependent on government money—foreign aid, in this case. That the leading experts in this field are almost unanimously in favor of more foreign aid is hardly a tribute to either the success of such aid abroad or the importance of it to American national interests. In other areas, such as social security or regional planning, the very expertise itself would be devalued if the programs were curtailed, and made worthless if they were discontinued. That the mass of expert opinion favors continuation of such programs is hardly a gauge of their value to the public.

In short, taxpayers pay billions of dollars to be brainwashed into supporting programs costing more billions. It is the political equivalent of a perpetual motion machine.

Stealing the Credit for Progress

LOS ANGELES HERALD EXAMINER / JANUARY 23, 1980

How do political reformers get away with continuing to use the whole population as guinea pigs, despite a trail of failures and broken promises that would embarrass a used-car dealer?

Whether it is the environmental protection racket today or the Prohibition amendment sixty years ago, it has been one disastrous "noble experiment" after another. It took us more than a decade to face the fact that Prohibition was not prohibiting. It was just corrupting. There are already studies showing that "environmental protection" doesn't protect the environment, that criminal "rehabilitation" programs don't rehabilitate, and that school "integration" programs don't integrate.

Like Prohibition, these other experiments did not simply fail. They have created massive new problems of their own. Prohibition was the greatest boost ever given to organized crime. We are still paying for that today. There are so many bureaucrats protecting the environment that it is literally a federal case to try to drill for oil, dig some coal, or build a hydroelectric dam. All the while, we keep wringing our hands over not having enough energy.

How do reformers and zealots keep getting away with these kinds of things—and keep getting new mandates to try their luck in new areas of our lives? They use two basic tactics. One tactic is to claim that their reforms would have worked if only there had been enough "commitment." That high-sounding word translates into English as more money and power. No matter how big a failure something is, you can always claim that it would have worked if only you could have drained the taxpayers some more, or had the power to tighten the screws on the public one more time.

The other tactic is for political reformers to steal credit for the progress created by others. There are grown men and women today who actually believe that without political crusaders we would still be living in the poverty of past eras. According to this vision, we would still be doing back-breaking toil at subsistence wages and living in shanties if it were not for forward-looking humanitarians. The fact that output per person has grown tremendously since those days is treated as incidental if it is mentioned at all. Our moral and political refusal to "accept" such poverty is credited with ending it.

But the real reason the poor no longer wear the rags and tatters that

42

were common in the nineteenth century is that a man named Singer invented the sewing machine. This machine mass-produced clothing and shoes so cheaply that they could be bought by the masses, brand new. Before that, second-hand clothing was what the poor wore, and diseases were spread throughout the large market for cast-off garments. Before the sewing machine, many Americans could not afford the luxury of shoes that were made differently for the left and right feet. In other countries, most working people could not afford shoes at all. In cold climates, they wrapped their feet in rags.

It was not our enlightened crusaders who brought light to the masses. It was Thomas Edison. It was not our intellectuals who ended the insularity of isolated communities. It was Henry Ford and the Wright brothers. For the man in the street, Kodak did more to make him aware of pictures than Rembrandt and all the museums put together. More people hear Beethoven as a result of recording than ever heard him in his own time.

It was not only mass production but mass distribution that put decent living and a few comforts in the life of the average person. The "middle-man" is often pictured as someone who just gets in between the producer and the consumer and collects his rip-off. But middlemen named Sears and Ward and Woolworth organized distribution in ways that cut costs. Mass markets were created for things people could not have afforded otherwise.

Our political deep thinkers and moral crusaders cannot believe that progress is not the fruit of their labors. They are like the rooster who conscientiously crowed and flapped his wings every morning and then retired to the yard, content that he had once more done his duty by making the sun rise.

Even those reformers who concede some credit to the economic system nevertheless believe that it would work "even better" with their "improvements" tacked on. But you cannot expect new Singers and Fords to do their jobs as well with a bunch of bureaucratic crusaders getting underfoot at every turn. There are very few games you can play at your best with kibitzers bugging you.

Status-Symbol Politics

THE WASHINGTON STAR / MARCH 27, 1978

Authorities in Canada's Quebec province provoked an international airline pilots' strike a couple of years ago by requiring pilots to converse with the control tower only in French. With hundreds of lives at stake when an airline pilot talks to the control tower, this seems like a strange place to indulge in arbitrary fiats. Yet it touches the heart of what is involved in status-symbol politics in various countries, including the United States.

What was involved in Quebec was (and is) the status of the French language and culture and, ultimately, the status of the French people who are the majority there. The English-speaking minority in Quebec has the skills, the property, the education, and all the good things of life that flow from them. The French Canadians have their pride—their wounded pride. Politics transforms all this into an emotional "issue" sufficiently powerful to endanger the lives of airline passengers from around the world. The weighing of costs against benefits seldom occurs in political struggles over status-symbol issues. Much of the "bilingualism" issue in the United States is status-symbol politics rather than a matter of tangible benefits to non-English-speaking groups. Just the opposite.

The average income of Hispanic Americans raised in homes where English was spoken is substantially higher than among those raised in homes where Spanish was the dominant language. There is nothing surprising about this. Anyone limited in his ability to communicate with the rest of the population is obviously at an economic disadvantage.

Considering how readily children pick up languages, a child from a Spanish-speaking home going to an English-speaking school would become bilingual as readily as millions of other immigrant children did in times past. Making the school itself bilingual may be far less effective in producing truly bilingual children. One of the most effective ways for anyone to learn a foreign language is to live surrounded by people who speak only that language. But such a logical approach is at odds with the heedless emotions of status-symbol politics.

Meaningful economic and social advancement takes too much time for ideologists, but symbolic victories can be achieved in the short run, so that is where their efforts are concentrated. Anyone who tries to understand the ferocity of the NAACP's school "integration" crusade of the past twenty years in terms of tangible benefits to black children will remain baffled. Wounded pride and symbolic "equality" are the touchstones of status politics. Cost-benefit analysis is the last thing crusaders want to hear.

It is probably futile to expect status-symbol addicts to kick the habit. What the rest of us can do is (1) avoid getting hooked ourselves; (2) insist that costs and benefits be weighed in public policy issues, instead of being swept along by rhetorical absolutes; and (3) carefully distinguish the views of "spokesmen" from the opinions of the people in whose name they presume to speak. This last is especially important. For example, polls show most blacks are opposed to both "busing" and "preferential" hiring or college admissions, but you would never guess this from listening to the NAACP.

Most of the people in whose name status crusaders claim to speak are in fact preoccupied with the age-old human problems of making a living, raising their children, and preserving their health and safety. The people themselves want tangible, not symbolic, advancement in terms of these goals. Only the more fortunate members of such groups, who have already achieved these things, can afford to ignore practical urgencies in favor of symbolic battles.

Status politics is a game for the affluent. As prosperity brings more and more people into the ranks of the affluent, we can expect to hear more and more status-symbol politics and the implacable irrationality that goes with it.

Political Programming
for All Exigencies

THE WASHINGTON STAR / MAY 28, 1979

While the rest of the world has moved forward into the age of computers, political announcements lag behind in the obsolete world of verbal statements and typed handouts. This is all the more surprising because the actual content of these statements and handouts is so standard that they could easily be programmed for a computer, perhaps by a trainee.

Take the elements of a typical political statement. First there is some situation, which the computer would have to be programmed to print out automatically as a *crisis*. Then there are the people affected by the situation, who would print out as the *victims*.

Next comes the *solution* to the crisis. A political solution is very easy to program. There are basically only three elements: more government activity, testimonials from intellectual partisans (printed out as *experts*), and more visibility for the politicians sponsoring it all.

A more or less basic computer print-out could be designed, with blanks to be filled in from the memory bank according to a few particulars of the issue at hand. The basic print-out might read something like this.

IN VIEW OF THE PRESENT _____ CRISIS AND THE GRAVE DANGERS IT REPRESENTS TO ALL AMERICANS, WE MUST VOICE OUR CONCERN, OUR COMPASSION, AND INDEED OUR COMMITMENT TO A SOLUTION. WE CANNOT STAND BY WHILE _____ ARE VICTIMIZED BY THIS TRAGIC AND OUTRAGEOUS _____.

MUCH AS WE MIGHT PREFER TO LEAVE _____ IN THE HANDS OF PRIVATE INDIVIDUALS, THE ECONOMIC MARKETPLACE, OR STATE AND LOCAL GOVERNMENTS, WE CANNOT DO SO. _____ IS A NATIONAL PROBLEM AND CALLS FOR A NATIONAL SOLUTION. THE FEDERAL GOVERNMENT MUST ASSUME THIS RESPONSIBILITY.

IN VIEW OF THE GREAT COMPLEXITY OF _____, WE ARE CALLING UPON ALL THE LEADING TALENTS IN THE FIELD OF _____ TO HELP US UNDERSTAND AND RESPOND TO IT. THESE EXPERTS WILL INCLUDE MEN AND WOMEN FROM PRIVATE INDUSTRY, THE UNIVERSITIES, GOVERNMENT, THE CHURCHES, AND INDEED FROM EVERY WALK OF LIFE ACROSS THIS GREAT NATION.

ONCE WE HAVE BROUGHT TOGETHER ALL THE KNOWLEDGE AND WISDOM WE CAN MUSTER, WE MUST THEN ACT, TO PUT AN END TO _____ AS A BLIGHT ON THE NATION AND PEOPLE.

IT WILL COST MONEY. NOTHING WORTHWHILE IS EVER FREE. BUT WE
INTEND TO KEEP COSTS TO A BARE MINIMUM, ONLY _____ BILLION
DOLLARS THE FIRST YEAR. [The computer will be programmed *not* to
project any subsequent year expenditures.] THAT IS LESS THAN THE
COST OF _____ INTERCONTINENTAL MISSILES. DEFENDING AMERICANS
FROM _____ IS JUST AS IMPORTANT AS DEFENDING THEM FROM
FOREIGN ENEMIES.

IN ORDER TO MAKE THIS A NATIONAL CONCERN AND A NATIONAL
COMMITMENT, WE INTEND TO KEEP THE AMERICAN PEOPLE FULLY
INFORMED AT EVERY STAGE OF THESE DEVELOPMENTS. WE WILL
REPORT ON NATIONAL TELEVISION AND THROUGH THE PRINT MEDIA,
AND HOLD PUBLIC MEETINGS IN CITIES ACROSS THE LAND.

WE INTEND TO SOLVE _____ IN OUR LIFETIME AND SO MAKE AMERICA
AN EVEN BETTER PLACE FOR OUR CHILDREN AND OUR CHILDREN'S
CHILDREN.

Obviously this would be easy to program for a computer. There would
not even need to be any programming for the logical consistency of what
is said. In many cases, it would be essential to leave that out.

Intellectuals
in China and America

LOS ANGELES HERALD EXAMINER / AUGUST 1, 1979

Chinese people have long been prosperous in many countries around the world, but not in China itself. How can the same intelligent and resourceful people, who have succeeded in the face of adversity from Indonesia to the Caribbean, be poverty-stricken in their native land?

Throughout the twentieth century, China has been a poor and backward country, pushed around in various ways by more technologically advanced nations, including tiny Japan at the turn of the century and in World War II. Japan is smaller than California, while China is larger than the United States. Imagine California sending an army out to conquer the rest of the United States and the United States having to call on other nations for help. That is how weak and disorganized China was.

It was not always this way in history, however. Centuries ago, China was the most technologically, intellectually, and organizationally advanced nation in the world. Thousands of years ago, China had an empire, industry, and literature, at a time when most Europeans were living a primitive tribal existence. As recently as the sixteen century, China had the highest standard of living in the world. What went wrong?

What went wrong in China is remarkably similar to what has been going wrong with the United States lately. Two classes rose to overwhelming dominance—bureaucrats and intellectuals. Both classes had always existed in the Chinese empire, but in the later dynasties they rose to completely eclipse such other competing elites as businessmen, the military, aristocratic families, or any others whose different viewpoints might balance or offset theirs.

Enormous emphasis was placed on holding degrees, and the government was run by people chosen for their ability to pass examinations. Confident that they were the brightest and the best, intellectuals and bureaucrats extended the power of government into every nook and cranny of the economy and society, telling everyone else what to do in every aspect of his life. They downgraded every other form of talent than the one they happened to possess. All of this was done in the name of neo-Confucian ideals that we would today call social justice.

After thousands of years of pre-eminence and advancement, China began to stagnate, fragment, and decline—just about the time that other nations were ready to enter the modern world. Members of the military were at the bottom of the intellectuals' pecking order, so it is hardly surprising that China was particularly vulnerable militarily. Invaders from other nations completed the process of destruction of China's greatness.

Chinese began emigrating en masse from their native land, seeking elsewhere the outlets for their talents that were no longer available in a China stifled by bureaucracy, corruption, and red tape. Some eventually turned in desperation to communism, little suspecting that it would in some ways be just more of the same, but with different rhetoric and symbols.

History doesn't have to repeat. But it does too often for comfort. Many of America's recent problems, internally and internationally, began with the rise to power of our own intellectual elite. Products of the massive increase in college attendance after World War II, these elites have flooded into the government, and much of the overflow goes into political crusades. For many, moral indignation has become a way of life, and telling others what to do has become a goal and a passion.

The more elite the colleges they come from, the more convinced they are that their right and duty is to whip the common herd into line through the power of government. Increasingly, they promote taking decisions out of institutions responsive to the people's dollars (business) or votes (elected officials), and putting these decisions into the hands of unelected judges, bureaucrats or so-called community organizations dominated by a few zealots like themselves.

Under the influence of our own intellectual-bureaucratic mandarins, we have seen prices and crime rates soar at home and the military security and political influence of the United States decline to new lows internationally. Like their counterparts in the old Chinese empire, they fail to see that a complex society needs the skills and experience of millions of people to run effectively. The arrogant presumptions of those with academic credentials is no substitute.

Suicidal Morality

LOS ANGELES HERALD EXAMINER / DECEMBER 19, 1979

The Duchess of Windsor once said that you can't be too rich or too thin (though some might say that she was both). In the post-Watergate era, many seem to think that you can't be too moralistic. But they are as wrong as the duchess.

There is very little danger that people's personal behavior will become too moral. The problem is when political decisions about the future are made as if they were moral decisions about the past. Political deep thinkers love to act as if they were God on Judgment Day. However, one of the little differences between them and God is that God doesn't have to worry about what is going to happen on the day after Judgment Day. But every decision a human being makes today is a decision he is going to have to live with tomorrow.

Recently, some political deep thinkers have criticized the admission of the shah of Iran to the United States. They see it as a moral question about his past, rather than a political question about our future. Whether we turn our backs on people who have been our allies today affects whether other people will be willing to be our allies tomorrow.

Often economic issues are approached in the same moralistic way—as if there were some predestined amount of output, and the only real question is dividing it up "fairly." But how much people can expect to make affects how much they are going to do. Every political scheme to keep prices down keeps production down. It is the same story whether the product is housing or oil today, butter and sugar during World War II, or chariots in ancient Rome.

Nowadays, you might think we would be concerned about our future supply of oil—especially domestically produced oil. But what arouses our moralists and politicians is preventing "windfall gains" by American oil companies. Denouncing oil company profit rates has become a national sport. Leading the denunciations are newspapers and television stations whose profit rates are two or three times those of the oil companies. And of course the biggest windfall gainers are politicians, who now have an extra couple of hundred billion in oil tax money to play around with.

Saving the public from being "exploited" by oil companies is the other half of the great moral crusade. But the cost of establishing the Department of Energy alone was equal to all the profits of all the oil companies

50

put together. The public doesn't save a dime that way.

"Ending our dependence on foreign oil" is the political slogan of the hour. But in practice that takes a back seat to preventing American-produced oil from selling at a price determined by supply and demand. It is already illegal to sell some American-produced oil at even half the price charged by the Organization of Petroleum Exporting Countries (OPEC). Better our money should go to the Arabs.

The public is led to believe that there is some physical deficiency of petroleum within our borders. But there are centuries' supply of petroleum here, and thousands of years' supply of natural gas. Our moral crusaders have simply made it legally difficult or impossible to get at most of it. Laws protect the frogs and the cactus. Price controls make much of our energy reserves unprofitable to develop. New England hasn't allowed a major new refinery to be built in the last twenty years—all the while demanding "adequate" heating oil at "reasonable" prices. The federal government would not dream of allowing American producers of natural gas to charge the kind of prices we readily pay to import it from Mexico or Canada.

What makes all this suicidal moralizing all the more ridiculous is that our lives are dominated by windfall gains and losses. Being born in this century rather than the last doubles your life span. Being born in America increases your income by ten or a hundred times what it would be in some other countries. Being born merely "normal" rather than brain-damaged is a windfall gain that makes economic inequalities pale into insignificance.

Selective indignation is reserved for the advantages and disadvantages that political crusaders have seized upon at the moment. Back when organized outrage was focused on the plight of the poor farmer, nobody cared that millions of people were catching hell because their skins were black. Later on, blacks were "in" and farmers were "out." Now whales are in and blacks are out. In a few years it will be something else. While the antinuclear crusade is in, every abstract possibility of harm from a nuclear power plant will get more headlines than a hundred men killed in coal mining or cutting down trees, or any other way of getting energy.

Moral crusades may create media excitement and give some people something to do. But preparing for our future should never be confused with playing God on Judgment Day.

Political Kibitzing

LOS ANGELES HERALD EXAMINER / NOVEMBER 21, 1979

This may go down in history as the golden age of kibitzers. There have always been kibitzers looking on from the sidelines, telling us what card to play or what move to make in checkers. Nowadays they are telling everybody what to do in everything. There is no such thing as building a house, hiring a worker, selling a product, or making any other decision without an army of kibitzers telling you what to do.

Almost any set of letters you can think of—EPA, ICC, EEOC, etc.—designates some set of feds whose job is to second-guess and overrule other people's decisions. Then come the unofficial kibitzers. There's Ralph Nader, Common Cause, the "no nukes" kooks, and many others with more indignation than information.

Kibitzers are often wrong, but never in doubt. When they are just kibitzing at parlor games, we at least have the satisfaction of knowing that eventually they will have to sit down and play. Then we can all see if they really have as much pent-up brilliance as they think they do. If the game is for money, we may even have the satisfaction of lending them the fare to get home at the end of the evening.

But most political kibitzers never have to sit down to play, much less with their own money at stake. For example, the Securities and Exchange Commission (SEC) decided to kibitz the Sambo's restaurant chain on their contracts with their individual restaurant managers. For years, Sambo's had been making money and growing and attracting new managers with these contracts. After SEC kibitzing made them change their contracts, Sambo's started losing managers and losing money. Recently, they had to borrow millions just to stay afloat. But nobody at the SEC lost a dime.

Nobody at the Department of Energy missed a paycheck during the worst of the gasoline lines. No bureaucrat ever has his pay docked when his kibitzing and red tape forces someone out of business and their employees lose their jobs. Kibitzing at other people's expense has become a way of life for many. Students find it more interesting than studying. Politicians find it more interesting than taking care of tax-payers' money. Many others find it more interesting than producing something themselves.

Above all, the courts have become the grand kibitzers of the whole society. They unblushingly tell you what to do with your children. They tell the police what kind of cops to hire, tell the universities what kind of profs to hire and what kind of students to admit. They redraw the map of voting districts if they feel like shifting the political balance toward groups that are more in vogue. The judges just wink at the Constitution and wing it. If they are wrong, there is usually not a thing you can do about it, even if you find out before the election. Federal judges aren't elected, and they are in for life.

How did we get to the point where so many decisions are being made by people who don't pay the consequences if they are wrong? After all, being wrong is an old habit of human beings, and we aren't anywhere close to breaking it. Basically, we got here by buying the idea that the kibitzers are somehow nobler or smarter than others. Their decisions are not considered tainted, like those of the businessman who collects if he is right and has to cash in his chips if he is wrong.

Considering how often human beings have been wrong, you would think there was some advantage in at least limiting how long they can go on being wrong. A businessman who builds hotels where the real demand is for office buildings, or who manufactures air conditioners when the real demand is for furnaces, cannot keep it up very long. But a judge who believes that crime is caused by poverty can keep turning hoodlums loose for decades. An unelected coastal commission or zoning board can stifle housing forever for the sake of swamps and frogs. There is no limit to how much inflation the Federal Reserve can create, no matter how many people's life's savings are destroyed by it.

Kibitzers did not get uncontrolled power by calling it by its right name. They got it by calling it a lot of other things—social justice, compassion, ecology, or whatever else they thought we would buy. Many were very sincere in believing themselves purer or brighter than the common herd. The leading kibitzers are products of selective colleges and universities. They have long been among the top 10 percent (or even 1 percent) among their classmates as they went through school. Within a very narrow slice of human knowledge and experience, they are indeed superior. What they fail to understand is that watchmakers, television repairmen, and trapeze artists have a similar superiority in their areas—and nobody lets them tell everybody else how to live their lives.

The naive pretensions of the kibitzers would be laughable if they were not so often tragic in their consequences. The inefficiencies caused by their meddling are overshadowed by the slow erosion of personal freedom that occurs as more and more decisions are taken out of our hands.

A Phantom Majority for the ERA?

THE WASHINGTON STAR / JULY 24, 1978

Zealots seldom provide the best examples of logic, but advocates of the ERA have created a new political principle that is unique in its irrationality. Failing to get the required three-fourths majority needed for a constitutional amendment, they are prepared to create a phantom majority.

It goes like this: some state legislatures have voted for or against ERA, and others have voted both for it and against it at different times. What the ERA advocates want is to freeze all the "yes" votes for all time and then allow unlimited time for the "no" votes to be changed to "yes."

Congress allowed seven years for this amendment to be passed or not passed—ample time to hear all the arguments and decide democratically. If we generalized the political principle advocated by ERA zealots, the Republicans could instantly claim an overwhelming majority of the seats in both houses of Congress, because an overwhelming majority of states have voted Republican at some time or other. Unfortunately for the Republicans, we still follow the old-fashioned way of counting majorities according to how people voted at a given time. Phantom majorities collected from different eras are still a little avant-garde as a general political principle.

In fairness to the ERA advocates, they don't want our whole political system changed to allow phantom majorities on all issues and all elections. They just want this change for themselves. More specifically, they want to win, and they don't care how they do it.

It is an open question under the Constitution whether a state that voted to ratify an amendment can change its mind and rescind its decision by a later vote against ratification. Depending upon how the Supreme Court might rule on this issue, every "yes" vote on any constitutional amendment could be set in concrete forever.

It is in the light of this provision that the unlimited extension of time being demanded for ERA assumes such importance. If it were simply a matter of letting the struggle go on, with both sides' votes continuing to be tallied at the same time, that would be a different ball game.

The demand for an opportunity to create a phantom three-fourths majority for ERA is part of a wider social vision that encompasses many other issues. In this more general vision, the self-anointed decide among themselves what is "really" right for society and then regard the democratic process as simply an obstacle to be overcome to prevent the common herd from impeding "progress."

This arrogant elitism is obvious not only in the social composition of such "movements," but in their substitution of vituperation for open controversy, and their patronizing notion of "educating" those who disagree with them. Like other such movements, ERA zealots speak confidently in the name of a constituency which has in fact repudiated them.

Polls have shown most women opposed to most of the agenda of "women's liberation"—more so than men. It is in keeping with this pattern that most of the opposition to ERA comes from women.

The literal words of the ERA are unlikely to be objectionable to Americans of either sex. Indeed, these words add nothing of substance to what is already in the fourteenth Amendment. Unfortunately, the history of recent years shows how easily words about equality of rights can be perverted to mean equality of results, or the mindless disregard of important differences among individuals and groups.

No one wants to deny left-handers equal rights (equal lefts?), but there are reasons why left-handers are overrepresented at first base and underrepresented at shortstop. More generally, equality of status is not the overriding consideration in all social decisions, because many important differences depend upon behavior rather than status.

A left-hander's behavior is different from a right-hander's; that is the basis for the whole distinction in the first place. Women differ from men not only in the obvious physical and sexual ways, but also in life expectancy, susceptibility and resistance to many diseases and afflictions, and in the way married couples divide their domestic responsibilities.

It has already been made illegal to take some of these behavioral differences into account (life expectancy, for example), and a constitutional mandate would unleash more crusaders, bureaucrats, and judges to wreak more havoc by exalting status over behavior—and over common sense.

Women have a lot to lose in any such quixotic crusades, because much of their contribution takes the form of intangible but essential inputs that show up in the rewards received by others—notably their husbands and children. The law has tried to recapture some of those contributions for her by imposing legal responsibilities on husbands and, to a lesser extent, children.

Status has superseded behavior in many areas without any explicit confrontation of the two decision-making considerations. In other words, we have bought many ideas because of the way they were packaged rather than because of their contents. If we really believed that status was more important than behavior, we would have homes for unwed fathers. In this day and age, perhaps it is best to hastily add that that is an illustration, not an agenda.

Abortions and the Poor

LOS ANGELES HERALD EXAMINER / MARCH 5, 1980

The emotion-laden issue of abortion brings out a flood of tortured logic, as emotional issues often do. The most recent legal battle, still going on, is over government payment for abortion.

Because the courts have ruled that women have a legal right to an abortion, some people have jumped to the conclusion that the government has to pay for it. You have a constitutional right to privacy, but the government has no obligation to pay for your window shades. You have a right to travel abroad, but you can't charge your air fare and hotel bills to Uncle Sam, unless you are junketing on government business.

Political deep thinkers like to say that you don't "really" have a right unless you have the money to exercise it. It sounds sophisticated, but it is sophisticated nonsense. It is especially ridiculous when you *do* have the money but choose to spend it on something else.

Abortions cost less than many other things that low-income people buy, either for cash or on credit. For example, about 30 percent of poverty-income people own a color television. Other poor people pay for other conveniences or amenities. That is and should be their privilege. It should also be the privilege of taxpayers.

A reasonable question could be raised as to whether it is in the taxpayers' interest to prevent another unwanted child from entering the world. The battered children of teenage mothers, as well as the high cost of welfare and crime, are arguments that could be made and weighed. But that is completely different from talking about someone's *right* to force other people to pay for her abortion.

The "right to life" people on the other side have their own lapses from logic. Each healthy adult produces thousands of cells capable of becoming human beings. What "right to life" do these untold billions of cells have? More than 99 percent of them will never see the light of day, whether there are abortions or not.

If I am dying of kidney failure, do I have a right to one of your kidneys, or to any other part of your body you could spare that would keep me alive? The closet totalitarians among us would say yes, but most others would say no. Even if we grant the right-to-life argument that an unborn baby has as many human rights as any adult citizen, what adult citizen has a right to draw upon someone else's body to survive?

It is murder to deliberately kill a baby that survives separation from

57

its mother, as well it should be. Once people can be killed merely because they are inconvenient, we have taken a long step back toward barbarism.

Some would say that it makes little difference in the end whether a baby dies from separation or dies from a deliberately lethal drug or other medical way of killing. This, too, is sophisticated nonsense. In the end, we will all be dead, one way or another—but no one files homicide charges with every burial. Why and how someone dies matters enormously in every other context. It matters for babies too. A woman's right to do what she wants with her own body is not a right to do what she wants with someone else's body.

There are no easy or happy answers when things reach the point where abortion is being considered. The question is whether we will face the tragic dilemma, or try to evade the painful issue by creating sweeping "rights" on one side or the other.

Disaster Aid

LOS ANGELES HERALD EXAMINER / FEBRUARY 27, 1980

After every tragic fire or flood that sweeps through an area, people are asked if they will leave. Most seem to stay. It is heartening as a sign of the human spirit. But it raises some economic questions about government disaster aid.

Most Americans want to help when someone has been hurt. Politicians who declare "disaster areas" and make government money available look like good guys. Ninety percent of the political art consists of ostentatious giving and surreptitious taking. But every cent that is given is also taken. On what grounds do you justify taking someone's money for help to someone else?

How do you justify taking money from a factory worker's paycheck to help rebuild someone's half-million dollar home in Malibu? It is one thing to help someone who has fallen victim to an unexpected disaster. It is something else to subsidize living where high risks are known in advance.

Middle- and upper-income people subsidize others, so sometimes they think it is their turn to get something. But this is crazy. If every subsidy justifies another subsidy, we are headed for a society where no one pays the cost of his own decisions. If the middle- and upper-income classes are paying too much to subsidize others, the answer is to cut taxes, not increase subsidies to the affluent.

Many people are confused by the particular form that a subsidy takes. That is why politicians give subsidies in so many different forms. But the form is not really what matters. If the government lends you half a million dollars at 3 percent when the market would charge you 13 percent, that is the same as giving you an outright gift of $50,000 a year.

Politicians would of course claim that the loans that were repaid "cost the taxpayers nothing." They might even have the gall to claim that the government made money on the loans—3 percent. Try telling that to an economist, a banker, or anyone else who gives any serious thought to it. Anytime the government borrows money at a high rate of interest and lends it at a low rate of interest, it loses money. That loss is a hidden subsidy.

Hiding subsidies in artificially low interest rates is an old political game. The Tennessee Valley Authority and many other government projects have looked "self-supporting" this way for years. Much of the complexity of government finance is nothing more than concealment of how much it is giving away.

People who want to live on scenic hillsides have every right to live on scenic hillsides—at their own cost and risk. There is no point debating the pros and cons of that life-style. They know what it is worth to them, better than any third party can know. And if it is not worth enough for them to pay the full cost, why is it worth it to a taxpayer who lives somewhere else?

Over the years, we have moved dangerously close to the position that anything worth doing at all is worth doing with a subsidy. That political policy may be more dangerous in the long run than even the fires, floods, and mud slides. It will mean that kidding ourselves has become a way of life.

We won't have one cent more after we are all subsidizing each other than we had before. We will have less, because our decisions no longer carry the full cost or benefits to the individual who makes them, and they will be made less carefully. More than that, we will have turned over more of our lives, and our freedoms, to bureaucrats.

Is the Gasoline Crisis Real?

LOS ANGELES HERALD EXAMINER / SEPTEMBER 26, 1979

No sooner did gasoline lines start appearing around the country than people began asking over and over, "Is there really a gasoline shortage?"

All sorts of rumors went around—gasoline was being poured into the ground; oil tankers were stalling for time in the ocean, waiting for prices to rise. You name it; somebody said it. Every time a rumor was tracked down and no evidence found, that only spurred more rumors. When the government's own pet suspicions were undermined by a Department of Energy report, that only led to a White House repudiation of the report and a new investigation by a new secretary of energy.

It was certainly true that there was no reduction of petroleum production as would explain the dramatic—and traumatic—change in the gasoline situation. But it was not really gasoline that was in short supply.

Even in the worst periods of the gasoline crisis, well over 90 percent of the usual amount of gasoline was sold in most places. You might spend a lot of time looking all over town for a filling station that was open, and exasperating hours waiting in gas lines, but you generally ended up with about as much gas as you normally bought.

What was there a shortage of, then? Time. In New York City, for example, the average filling station was open 110 hours a week in September 1978, but only 27 hours a week in June 1979. With a 75 percent reduction in hours of service, it became much harder to find gasoline *when and where you wanted it*—even if you eventually found it somewhere else and hours later.

What happened is an old economic story—not peculiar to the oil industry, and not due to "dependence on foreign oil" or "an era of limits" or any other political cliches. Similar things have been happening for centuries when price controls have been put on products, whether domestic or imported, natural resources or man-made objects.

Due to the complexities of gasoline price controls, they only took full effect gradually over time, and in the Spring of 1979 they took effect with a vengeance. A central problem with price controls is trying to define the product that is being controlled. The complexities of the real world almost always defeat the words used in the law. For example, when apartment rents are controlled, the number of apartments may not change in the short run, but all the auxiliary services that the

61

tenant expects usually decline or disappear. Maintenance, heat, hot water, painting, etc., are reduced by the landlord, so that the actual product—the apartment—is no longer the same.

In the case of gasoline, the service stations' hours are a crucial part of the product, as we discovered all too vividly. Price controls not only reduced filling station profit margins, they led to more gasoline being demanded than supplied. The filling stations had both an incentive and an opportunity to save on labor costs by cutting back hours. They sold all their gas continuously for a few hours a day, instead of being open for motorists to drive in sporadically at their convenience at times throughout the day and night.

From the point of view of the economy, what was saved were a few man-hours of filling station workers' time, and what was wasted were many more man-hours of motorists' time, searching and waiting for gas. Economies that have more product prices controlled, or more government "planning" in general, also have waiting lines as a common fact of life.

Once the government is in the act, however, it can never simply withdraw and let things go back to normal. However beneficial that might be to the public, it would be a political disaster for the powers that be, because it would reveal that politicians were the problem rather than the solution.

Instead, politicians have to find some villain the public can hate— OPEC, the oil companies, James Schlesinger. All of these being ultimately human beings, there will necessarily be many things they have done that can be criticized. But that is very different from saying that they caused the gas lines. Shortages have followed price controls at least as far back as Hammurabi's code, more than three thousand years ago. When will we ever learn?

Terrorist Celebrities

THE WASHINGTON STAR / AUGUST 9, 1978

Many who described the brutal murder of Italian Premier Aldo Moro as a "senseless" act that did Italy's "red brigade" itself no good missed the point entirely. And it is a point that is important well beyond this one tragic and shocking episode.

For several weeks a group of obscure young men became important. They carried out a deed that made headlines around the world. They had a famous man in their power, to abuse or taunt as they pleased and to kill when they felt like it. They saw the life of the country around them disrupted as police, workers, and others changed their daily routines in response to the event. The pope, the American president, and the United Nations recognized them with appeals and declarations. In normal times, they might never have gotten past the secretaries to see any of these people, much less expect to influence them. With one daring crime, they leapfrogged bureaucracy and protocol and elbowed their way into the headlines and even into history.

By focusing solely on the ostensible "cause" for which the red brigade was fighting, we missed the crucial point that their personal reward for terrorism was immediate and massive, regardless of what effect it has on the long-run prospects of their cause. The red brigade's ideology or goal is vague and elusive,—like that of the Bader-Meinhof gang in Germany or the Weatherman bombers in the United States.

A systematic thinker like Karl Marx would probably turn over in his grave if he could hear the little scraps of rhetoric and fragments of thought that serve as an ideological fig leaf for all this hell raising. Marx was scathing in his criticisms of contemporary radicals for whom "revolutionary" activity was an ego trip. He also pointed out that it was especially the children of the rich who played such games. A hundred years later, it is still much the same story.

The media and the intellectuals tend to judge terrorists in terms of the effects of their acts on what the terrorists themselves define as their cause—the "avenging" of this or the "liberation" of that. Usually the terrorists' acts don't have a ghost of a chance of achieving their proclaimed goals, but they can give a lot of importance to a lot of otherwise insignificant people in the meantime. And these are not merely insignificant individuals: they are often insignificant individuals who grew up surrounded by people with wealth, power, or recognition which they

63

would be unable to duplicate through normal channels for many long years.

Some young people in this awkward situation simply "drop out" and pursue a different kind of life, sometimes loftily dismissing what they could not achieve for a long time anyway. But if some find the game not worth the candle, others decide that they will play the game by their own rules and win big quick.

Terrorism does it, and it does it in part because the rest of us take their rhetoric and poses seriously instead of seeing it as criminal activity by people who put their egos above other people's lives. From this perspective, it should not be surprising that so many of these terrorists turn out to be spoiled rich kids.

The importance of importance extends well beyond contemporary terrorists. People struggle, push, lie, and betray to become important. Down through the centuries, countries have been devastated, atrocities committed, and millions of innocent lives destroyed in order that a handful of people could feel important. It is naiveté, almost to the point of criminal negligence, to blithely ignore all this and judge each person or activity solely in terms of what is claimed to be the goal.

Even in much more conventional political activity, the importance of importance as a motivating force should not be underestimated. The extension of government power over the individual, and the gobbledy-gook that accompanies it, can hardly be understood without understanding that both things make people important.

Programs that fail in their avowed aims may nevertheless be wholly successful in giving importance to bureaucrats, legislators, or judges. Proliferating laws may strangle the legal system and clog the courts, but every bill has at least one name on it as sponsor and therefore provides an opportunity to get that name in the newspapers. No one ever made a career or a place in history by letting the ordinary citizen use his own best judgement. In that simple fact is contained one of the greatest dangers to freedom—in the long run, more dangerous than terrorists.

A Guilt-Edged Society

LOS ANGELES HERALD EXAMINER / OCTOBER 17, 1979

An old advertising slogan said, "Progress is our most important product." Nowadays, guilt is our most important product. And it is selling like hotcakes.

Every American newspaper, magazine, or television station denounces our sins regularly. Everything that isn't as good as they want it to be is our fault—whether it is illiteracy among the Eskimos, the standard of living in Portugal, or the dwindling number of exotic birds in the swamps. We have become a guilt-edged society.

And we are *all* guilty. They won't accept any alibi that you were somewhere else at the time of the crime. Even if you were out back cutting the grass, or working late at the office, or were laid up in bed with the flu, it is somehow still your fault. And it won't do any good, for example, to say that you have nothing against exotic birds, or even that some of your best friends are exotic birds. You are still guilty.

How did we get to be guilty of so many things, especially when we thought that we were busy trying to make a living or take care of the household? Well, it all depends on how you look at it. The way the deep thinkers, moral crusaders, and miscellaneous messiahs look at it, good things just happen; bad things are caused by our sins.

For example, if our homes are well heated in the winter, that just happens. But if whoever dug the coal or drilled the oil well to provide that heat happened to inconvenience some wild animals or produce an unsightly hole in the ground, no matter how far out in the boondocks, that is sin. If Americans produce a greater abundance of material necessities, conveniences, and comforts than people in other countries, that just happens. But if we then consume more of "the world's" production than other countries, that is sin.

Only our most highly educated people think this way. The ordinary factory worker, secretary, or waitress understands perfectly well that things have costs. They are not the least bit shocked when the water that people drink in Los Angeles causes the lake that it comes from to have less water in it.

Those who are shocked, outraged, and demonstrating over it are people who have been sent through college and graduate school—largely with tax money from factory workers, secretaries, and waitresses. It is those who have always been given 90 percent of what they want who are bitter over not getting the other 10 percent. It is they who are ready to chuck it all, go off and follow some movement, guru or (in extreme cases) Jane Fonda.

If such people want to "do their own thing," that may just be part of the human comedy. The tragedy is when they do the rest of us in, in the process. They have made it a tremendously expensive hassle to try to build housing, drill for oil, generate electricity, or even protect our lives against criminals or Soviet nuclear forces.

Some people can get what they want just by asking for it—or by demanding it—from guilty parents, gutless school officials, or politicians eager to please everyone. The whole society cannot follow their example, however much they urge us to join their protests and demonstrations. Somebody is going to have to pay for every speck of benefit. That somebody is going to be the average American, as long as they can make us feel guilty over using the land for people, rather than frogs or weeds.

It is easy to look down your nose at mere material progress, after it has relieved you from toil and insulated you from the harsh realities of nature in the raw. For the poor still hoping to share some of those benefits, it is a different ball game. Those jam-packed into city apartments and tenements could have a little more elbowroom if the government were not holding about a third of the total land of the country off the market. An area equal to all of the United States east of the Mississippi River is being "preserved" for the benefit of a handful of birdwatchers and backpackers, who can have their weekend Waldens at the taxpayers' expense. The physicians, dentists, engineers, college professors, and students who are the chief beneficiaries of "environmentalism" could well let guilt begin at home.

It is easy to denounce spending on military power as "waste" when you are safely insulated from the consequences of not having it. The value of military power is much better appreciated by those who don't have it: the people currently being exterminated by the Communists in Cambodia, the East Germans who have risked their lives (and their children's lives) trying to make their way past the Berlin Wall, the refugees from Vietnam who have put their families on leaky boats and sailed off to an unknown fate.

In the nineteenth century, slaves who greeted the Union army that ended their bondage had a very different view of the military than our sheltered elites today. So too did the Europeans of a generation ago who greeted the American Army that came to end the long nightmare of

Nazi occupation. Here, as elsewhere, it is only the privileged who can despise the sources of their privileges.

As for the rest of us, we can remember that when something doesn't sell, it is not going to keep on being produced. Not even guilt.

3

ECONOMIC POLICY

ECONOMICS IS BASICALLY the study of what is not possible with given resources. The problem is that what we want is always more than what is possible. That is where politics comes to the rescue. Politics has been called the art of the possible, but it is really the art of the *plausible*. Economics deals with what you can actually achieve. Politics deals with what you can get people to believe. The reason that politics usually wins out over economics is that economics is limited to what is possible. A good politician can always do better than that—or appear to, in the short run. In the long run, we discover inflation, shortages, unemployment, and many other consequences of political "benefits." But this only sets the stage for a new round of political solutions to our economic problems.

The essays that follow try to focus on the basics of economics that often get ignored in the rush to do good or to make everyone happy at once. None of this is difficult to understand intellectually. What is difficult is to break the emotional habits that make us ignore reality in the first place. Those habits are all too human. They have led to similar economic policies—and similar disasters—in various countries around the world and at various times in history, going back thousands of years.

The Facts of Economic Life

LOS ANGELES HERALD EXAMINER / SEPTEMBER 19, 1979

Asking people where prices come from gets more embarrassing answers than asking small children where babies come from. It is not nearly as funny, however, because adults vote on economic policy—and some vote in Congress.

Many people think that high prices come from greed, while low prices come from sellers being reasonable, humane, responsible and other Boy Scout virtues. It is the economic equivalent of believing that the stork brought you. Even those who have been told "the facts of life" about supply and demand can drift back into believing that rents go up because landlords are greedy and food prices rise because supermarkets are ripping us off.

If prices were determined by the arbitrary will of sellers, it would be hard to explain why they fall into such regular patterns. For example, housing costs in Los Angeles generally rise as you go west, toward the ocean, and fall as you go east, toward the smog. Greed must increase as you get near fresh air and decrease as you get into the smog. Who would have thought that smog had such moral benefits?

As for supermarkets, they average about a dime of profit on ten dollars' worth of groceries. Even if they were in business just for their health, this would still have very little effect on grocery prices. They make their money on volume, not markup.

Prices convey information about what is scarce or plentiful, what is hard or easy to make, what is an efficient or inefficient way to do things. When prices convey information that people don't want to hear, they are quick to blame somebody. Motorists in Boston believe that their unusually high auto insurance rates are a plot by the insurance companies. Anyone who has seen Boston drivers in action will find nothing mysterious about their high auto insurance rates. If you want to see a car changing lanes in a tunnel or challenging an emergency vehicle for the right of way at an intersection, go to Boston—and watch from a safe distance.

High prices in low-income neighborhoods bring out the moral crusaders in force. It does no good to tell them about the high crime rates in such neighborhoods and its effect on the cost of operating a store. They just know that sinister forces are exploiting helpless victims. But why "greedy" store owners are leaving poor neighborhoods is a puzzle, if that

70

is where they are reaping big profits.

Politicians encourage us to believe these moral theories of prices. Then they can play the knights in shining armor, rescuing us from economic dragons and living happily ever after in Washington. Rent control, wage-price guidelines, interest-rate ceilings—these are all political ways of soothing the symptoms of facts we do not want to face, such as the scarcity of housing or inflationary government deficits. As with other treatments of symptoms, the disease itself often gets worse. Rent control is a proven way to create and maintain a housing shortage. Interest rate ceilings, to help the poor, force the poor to resort to loan sharks, who ignore the legal limits of interest and have their own ways of collecting.

Perhaps the biggest reason why politicians want us to believe that prices are determined by greed is that they don't want the voters to blame them for the inflation that always follows in the wake of continued government deficits. Better we should be mad at the butcher, the baker, or the candlestick maker. Hence the psychodrama of the president coming on television to sternly warn those who raise prices, while the government keeps printing money as fast as the presses will turn. The only way prices will come down is if the Bureau of Engraving runs out of green ink—or the Office of Management and Budget stops using red ink. Neither of these things is very likely.

Price Controls

LOS ANGELES HERALD EXAMINER / JUNE 13, 1979

When something that has been happening for four thousand years happens again, how surprised should we be?

A recent study shows that price controls have appeared and disappeared in history for more than forty centuries. What is even more remarkable is how the same results—shortages—always follow price controls, whether what is being regulated is wheat, housing, or gasoline. Gasoline lines not only go down the block. They go back in history.

More than a thousand years before the birth of Christ, the Chinese empire followed policies that are as contemporary as the Carter administration's. They created vast amounts of paper money and then expressed surprise and shock that prices were rising. Their solution, of course, was not to cut government spending but to control prices and regulate the economy. When this only led to further economic disasters, the ancient Chinese at least had the good sense to stop.

Inscrutable Westerners, however, have often taken the position that every failure of controls is a reason for more and stronger controls. These shortages are then blamed on the "greed" of the sellers. Long before there was ever a single oil company, shortages were denounced by politicians as being the fault of the sinister machinations of the producers.

The Roman emperor Diocletian denounced the "avarice" of merchants and speculators as piously as Jimmy Carter—while inflating the currency, raising the taxes on middle and working class, supporting vast numbers of idle people at government expense, and engaging in grandiose spending schemes. The price of gold also skyrocketed, then as now. Diocletian insisted that "justice" required the government to intervene in the economy, and set the prices of everything from beer to silk. Suddenly, there was a shortage of everything from beer to silk. It so happened that Diocletian lasted only four more years as emperor after issuing his price control edicts. 1980 will tell just how far history will go in repeating itself.

An even closer parallel to our present gasoline fiasco has occurred again and again in places facing famines. Whenever there has been a crop failure or a city under seige, politicians have rushed to the rescue with price controls, to prevent "windfall gains" by sellers of food. These laws do not produce a speck of food, but are regarded as noble and

72

humanitarian. Like other price controls, they reduce supply—and in this case, that means unnecessary starvation.

When the city of Antwerp was blockaded by the Spaniards in the sixteenth century, food prices rose just as gasoline prices rose after OPEC cut off petroleum to twentieth-century America. In both cases, the government kept the prices down, reducing the incentives to economize. In Antwerp, "the city lived in high spirits until all at once the provisions gave out." Sound familiar?

In both cases, hostile foreign action was not as destructive as domestic politics. Before price controls, all suppliers of food had an incentive to ship food to beseiged Antwerp, even through the Spanish blockade. Once prices were kept down to "reasonable" and "just" levels, no one in his right mind was going to send food shipments through a military blockade for the same price he could get by selling in complete safety elsewhere. Starvation forced Antwerp to surrender. They had blockaded themselves more effectively than the Spanish navy had.

We are currently blockading ourselves from the energy we need more effectively than OPEC has. The amount of petroleum and coal within our own borders is enough to last for centuries. There is enough natural gas to last for thousands of years. But there is no amount of abundance that cannot be ruined by politicians.

How are we blockading ourselves from energy? Let me count the ways. Price controls and mountains of red tape are the most obvious way to create a shortage of anything, regardless of how much of it exists in nature. Eighteenth-century France was the leading agricultural nation in Europe when its people were starving under the idealistic price-control laws passed after the French Revolution. If politicians regulated the Sahara desert, they would end up having to import sand.

In addition, every self-righteous recreational interest group that chooses to call its members environmentalists can block drilling, refining, hydroelectric dams, or anything else that might spoil its fun. Even if an oil pipeline or a surface coal mine is miles out in the boondocks, a handful of backpackers might be annoyed to see it. Or it might endanger some weed or reptile that most of us have never heard of, but which has become the sacred cow of some environmental sect, or the ward of some bureaucracy, or the darling of some court.

If the energy is nuclear, it is presumed guilty until proven innocent. A rare nuclear accident that gives people nearby as much radiation as they would get from a set of dental X rays is widely described as a "disaster" and brings the Ralph Naders and Jane Fondas out of the woodwork in force.

Every new revelation that oil companies are in business to make

73

money (like everyone else) is treated as a shocking exposé, even by newspapers and television stations with even higher profit rates. That some oil company profits are being invested in other industries which are not so bedeviled by red tape is taken as another condemnation of oil companies—not of red tape.

This kind of economic reaction to government intervention has also happened elsewhere, and recently. The Egyptian government has decided that bread is important to its people, just as the U.S. government has decided that petroleum is important. In both cases, this reasonable beginning is followed by the political conclusion that government control is needed. As bureaucracy and red tape have built up around the production of bread in Egypt, Egyptian bakers have started putting more and more of their efforts into producing pastries, which involves less red tape.

The result is that bread is harder to find, leaving the poor worse off, while those who can afford pastries can follow Marie Antoinette's advice to "eat cake" during a bread shortage. It is fascinating to read a book like *Forty Centuries of Wage and Price Controls* [Robert L. Schuettinger and Eamonn F. Butler (Caroline House, 1979)]. But do we actually have to relive every mistake in history?

What is a Billion Dollars?

LOS ANGELES HERALD EXAMINER / AUGUST 29, 1979

One of the reasons government spending has shot up through the roof is that the very units in which it is measured are so incomprehensible to so many people. What does a "billion" dollars mean except, vaguely, "a lot of money"? If someone had been spending a thousand dollars a day every day since the birth of Christ, they would not yet have spent a billion dollars. In the year 2000, they would still have about $270 million to go. That is how vast a billion dollars is.

Last year the federal government spent more than $500 billion. To get a picture of what that means, imagine that instead of spending a measly thousand dollars a day, someone had been spending a half-million dollars a day every day since the birth of Christ. The total amount spent in all these centuries would add up to less than the federal government spent in 1978 alone.

No government has the guts to come right out and tax people enough to pay these kinds of bills, so it runs up inflationary deficits instead. The Internal Revenue Service (IRS) may take a big bite, but that's literally not the half of it.

A major part of the financial expertise of government consists of devising ways to conceal how much they are taking from the public. Those who complain that the government is not supporting the creative arts have just never looked at federal bookkeeping.

One gimmick is to call some expenditures "loans" or "loan guarantees." No one in his right mind expects New York City to repay its "loans," except with more loans. But right now the account books look good—and right now is what counts in politics.

Another gimmick is to call a big chunk of our taxes by the name of "contributions" to Social Security. The image is of a fund accumulating somewhere to pay us in our old age. Don't you believe it! An image closer to reality would be Uncle Sam taking our "contribution" money out of the incoming morning mail and sending it out in the afternoon mail to people on Social Security. It is just another disguised tax used to cover current spending. When we get old enough to draw Social Security, whatever we get will depend on how much the government takes from the people still working then. And whether it comes through IRS or the Federal Insurance Contributions Act (FICA) is a matter of bureaucratic detail and political sleight of hand.

Still, all the fancy bookkeeping in the world cannot equal plain old inflation for fooling the public. Deficit spending and inflation mean that the government takes goods and resources from the public indirectly instead of by taxes. Economically, it is pretty much the same thing either way. But politically, the more you can hide what is happening, the more you can get away with taking.

One of the best ways to hide anything is to direct people's attention to something else. Magicians have known this for ages. When the government creates deficits and expands the money supply to cover it, prices rise. It's been happening that way for thousands of years. Yet each time it happens the government acts surprised, hurt, and indignant. Inflation is blamed on "greedy" businessmen, "irresponsible" labor unions, and sometimes mean landlords, grasping bankers, and other villains to suit the occasion.

To put itself on the side of the angels, the government rebukes, entreats, or threatens these terrible people who are raising prices, while the government's printing press is running full blast, turning out money, in the background. The president comes on television, looking grave and moral. His subordinates look purposeful as they go rushing off in all directions to find the villains, who went thataway.

It's a great show. It's had a longer run than *South Pacific*. However, even *South Pacific* finally had to close. Proposition 13 and its spreading influence across the nation suggest that we may have finally seen this show as many times as we can take.

Kicking the Big-Spending Habit

THE WASHINGTON STAR / n.d.

After half a century of almost constant deficits by the federal government, a desperate effort is being made to stop this trend with a constitutional amendment requiring a balanced budget. Twenty-eight state
legislatures have already voted to have a constitutional convention
called for that purpose. Another six states, and a convention will have to
be called for the first time since 1787.

Washington politicians and pundits, who have calmly accepted the
deficits and the runaway inflation for nearly two generations, are suddenly in hysteria over the thought of a constitutional convention. All
sorts of reasons are given why a budget cannot be balanced. All sorts of
terrible things are predicted if a constitutional convention is called. The
Bill of Rights could be repealed, for starters, according to alarmed
big-spending politicians and their media friends. Despite all the Washington mumbo-jumbo, balancing the federal budget is hard for basically
one reason: it is popular to give people things from Uncle Sam and
unpopular to raise taxes.

Before this political trend took hold back in the 1930s, balanced
budgets were the rule rather than the exception. Every federal budget
in the 1920s either was balanced or had a surplus. Throughout the
nineteenth century the federal government finished in the black far
more often than it finished in the red.

Balancing the budget is not some mysterious problem that we have to
wait for a genius to solve. It was done for a long time before the New Deal
discovered the political magic of winning votes with giveaways without
losing votes with tax increases. The great political success of that
formula has led to its continued use and expansion ever since.

Kicking that habit is the problem. The relationship between government deficits and inflation is very clear, despite all the quibbles that can
be made by big spenders and their political allies. We have gotten so
used to inflation that we have come to think of it as somehow inevitable.

But throughout the 1920s, there were no significant increases in the
general price level. Then came the era of big spending. The price level
more than doubled between the 1930s and the 1950s. It doubled again
between the mid-1950s and the mid-1970s. And the end is not yet in
sight.

Economic "experts" have told us that a balanced budget is just a fetish. Special circumstances may even make it undesirable at times. But history tells us that once politicians are free from the need to balance the budget, the sky is the limit. The "special circumstances" that economists talk about become a fetish. Such circumstances seem to be happening almost all the time, for most of the last 50 years. *Crisis* has become a routine word.

We can always leave room for genuine emergencies by allowing Congress to authorize an unbalanced budget with a two-thirds or three-fourths majority. We don't need to leave them a blank check, the way we do now.

Some people argue that a constitutional amendment is not the best way to limit federal spending. Since we obviously haven't yet discovered any other effective way, why wait until we think of the perfect way before doing anything? One approach does not preclude other approaches as well.

The second aspect of the current political attacks on a constitutional convention to limit spending are the bogeyman fears that are being whipped up. Some big spenders picture the Bill of Rights being repealed, the Supreme Court abolished, and Congress handcuffed. All this hysteria ignores one simple fact. Whatever a constitutional convention proposes, all the states have to vote on it, and two-thirds have to agree in order for the proposal to become "the law of the land."

It is true that there are many things the American people resent besides inflationary deficits, and some of these might also be considered by a constitutional convention. But after decades of quiet acceptance of power grabs by appointed federal judges taking over the functions of elected representatives, and anonymous bureaucrats issuing more laws than Congress, it is ironic to see this sudden panic at the thought of government of the people, by the people, and for the people.

Paul Revere won fame by sounding the alarm "The British are coming!" Today's big spenders and paternalists are sounding the alarm because the Americans are coming.

Phony Prices

LOS ANGELES HERALD EXAMINER / NOVEMBER 2, 1978

How much does it cost for something you can't get? How much wages do you earn when you are not working at all?

Sound like a riddle with a trick answer? Actually, these are some of the most serious questions in our economic and political life. They are questions that ought to be asked of every politician who poses as a champion of the people by advocating controls over prices, wages, or rents.

Such controls have existed, off and on, for literally thousands of years. They were tried in ancient China, Babylon, and Rome; in the Middle Ages; in eighteenth-century France; in World War II America, and at one time or another on every continent. The results have been the same everywhere. When the price is artificially lowered, a shortage results. When the price is artificially raised, a surplus results. Whether it is minimum-wage laws, rent control, farm parity prices, or interest rates ceilings, the results are the same: the one who is favored by the way the price is legally set, whether it be buyer or seller, finds that he can't get what he wants at the artificial price.

In innumerable times and places, minimum-wage laws have reduced job opportunities for low-skill workers, farm "parity" prices have led to agricultural surpluses, rent control has produced housing shortages and slums, and "reasonable" limits on interest rates have made it harder for people to get loans at all. Political memories are short, however, and so these schemes get resurrected again and again, literally down through the centuries. One reason is that it takes time for all the consequences to unfold, and politicians are elected in the short run. By the time the housing in a nice middle class neighborhood has deteriorated into hopeless slums (as under rent control in New York), the original champion of thepeople has gone on to bigger and better things, perhaps on the national political scene.

As long as transactions are voluntary, prices are just terms on which people agree to trade some things for other things. Whether it is labor or housing, milk or bank loans, the sellers would prefer to charge more and the buyers would prefer to pay less. But the actual price is what they can agree on, rather than pass up the transaction altogether. When the politician intervenes to change the price for one side's benefit, the other side becomes less interested in the transaction. Depending on how far the price is artificially raised or lowered, the supply or the demand may completely disappear. In this case, the price is completely phoney. It shows what you *would* pay *if* you could get what you want.

Rents are very low on rent-controlled apartments in New York, as anyone can discover when they walk around for weeks or months trying vainly to find one vacant. The jobs that unemployed teenagers don't have pay well. The loan that someone needs and can't get usually has a very reasonable interest rate. Depending on how desperately he needs the money, he may have to go to a loan shark, who ignores the law when he makes the loan and uses his own strong-arm collection methods. The natural gas that would have kept people from literally freezing in the Northeast last winter was very inexpensive in the gas-producing states, thanks to federal price controls—so low that people within those states were using the gas for heating their swimming pools and other low-priority uses, while people in the colder states were losing business, jobs, and sometimes even their lives for lack of fuel.

All these nice low prices, courtesy of politicians, were phony prices. They were the prices of something that many people couldn't get. Do politicians know what they are doing when they advocate price-fixing schemes that seem to promise something for nothing? Some do, some don't. Hammurabi was embarrassed to discover that supplies to the markets were declining after his price fixing schemes were imposed about three thousand years ago. Many people still remember the many shortages that existed during the comprehensive price controls of World War II, though they may have considered the two things coincidental.

No doubt if rent control becomes a permanent way of life in Los Angeles, the deterioration of housing, decline of apartment construction, and rising conversions to condominiums will be regarded by many as coincidental. But by then it will have given a boost to the careers of miscellaneous political saviors, so it will be a success from their stand-point—however much the rest of us end up losing as a result of their grandstand humanitarianism.

"Inflation Fighting" or Show Biz?

LOS ANGELES HERALD EXAMINER / AUGUST 5, 1979

Anyone who has been keeping score on the fight against inflation must know that inflation has won most of the rounds and scored several knockdowns already. Inflation has a winning streak that goes back for decades. In some countries it goes back for centuries.

How did inflation get to be so unbeatable? Very simple. Most of its fights are not for real. The government has no intention of cutting its own spending, or balancing the budget, or stopping the printing presses from turning out money.

If we are not really going to fight inflation, why do we keep staging these bouts? For the same reason that there are professional wrestling matches: people love a good show, with heroes and villains and lots of grunting and making faces—even if the punches don't land and the falls are fake.

Like professional wrestling, inflation fighting is much easier to understand as show biz than as a serious contest. It was entirely appropriate that President Ford's version of inflation fighting had buttons that said WIN (Whip Inflation Now) and a theme song composed by Meredith Wilson. If only they had added 76 trombones, he might have been re-elected, but such are the might-have-beens of politics.

President Carter's inflation-fighting show began with the usual predictions of victory, much in the style of Ford's WIN button or the bold and grandiloquent prefight statements of wrestlers. There was even a photograph of Alfred Kahn and other members of the administration's anti-inflation "team" wielding baseball bats as they prepared to go to bat against inflation. Ordinarily, a picture of middle-aged men in business suits holding baseball bats would be considered ridiculous, but a certain amount of audience indulgence is essential for all forms of show business—particularly at that end of the spectrum where you find circuses, professional wrestling, and inflation fighting.

The show business of politics is not art for art's sake. After all the heady rhetoric, torchlight parades, and "spontaneous" demonstrations, the bottom line is—will it win votes? Once we understand that the real purpose of "fighting" inflation is to win elections, then many things fall into place that might otherwise just seem bizarre.

First there is the big publicity buildup of inflation as a tough opponent, much like the buildup of Gorgeous George, a sort of Liberace of

PINK AND BROWN PEOPLE

the wrestling ring who used to pack them in to watch his "fights." In point of fact, inflation has been beaten easily by any opponent who was serious. Whenever there have been sustained periods of balanced budgets, inflation has been beaten cold. The last decade of balanced budgets was the 1920s, and the price level at the end of the decade was no higher than at the beginning. The last century with more federal budgets in black than in red was the nineteenth century, and the price level at the end of that century was no higher than at the beginning.

Today, try to imagine prices remaining stable even for three years! If you have that much imagination, you can write science fiction. After you have written another *Star Wars*, try writing a balanced budget and getting Congress to pass it. Congress is scared stiff at the thought of a constitutional amendment that would force them to balance the budget—the way innumerable Congresses used to do year after year.

The political purpose of inflation fighting is not to fight inflation, but to give the voters someone to blame for inflation—someone outside of government. However futile this may be as a means of keeping prices down, it is often a political success in casting government officials as heroes (inflation fighters) and others as villains ("greedy " businessmen, "irresponsible" unions, etc.). In these political or show business terms, inflation fighting is a big hit—which is why it is always coming back in reruns, just like *The Wizard of Oz* or *Gone with the Wind*.

After building up inflation as a tough villain of a fighter, it is necessary to build up some white hope who will take him on. The present incumbent, Alfred Kahn, is always referred to as the administration's "chief inflation fighter." It is a wonder (and a blessing) that he does not appear in Indian headdress. What is ironic is that he comes directly from the Civil Aeronautics Board (CAB), where he argued the benefits of decontrolling prices in the airline industry. Now he is apparently trying to control them everywhere else. Politics requires a certain "versatility of convictions," to use Veblen's phrase, and Kahn is nothing if not versatile.

Most people aren't aware that Alfred Kahn, in addition to having been a CAB commissioner and a professor of economics, was also a performer in Gilbert and Sullivan musicals. He is obviously the perfect man for the job of "inflation fighting."

Rent Control

LOS ANGELES HERALD EXAMINER / DECEMBER 12, 1979

Do we want more housing or more moralizing about housing? Apparently our politicians want more moralizing about housing. Rent control and condominium conversion are the order of the day, from Los Angeles to Washington, D.C.

Clamping price control and red tape on any product is a surefire way to create and maintain a shortage of it. Rent control has produced housing shortages from New York to Paris to Hong Kong. Sometimes the public learns from bitter experience, and eventually the rent control is repealed. Often it takes decades of increasingly overcrowded and deteriorating housing to pour cold water on political enthusiasm for rent control. But then, after a new political generation comes along, the same old notion can turn up again and once more arouse political passions. We are in one of these cycles now.

Why don't rent controls work? Basically, because people will do more when they receive more, and do less when they receive less. When housing prices are high, everybody and his brother tries to build more housing. When there's no money in it, people find something else to build (offices, motels, etc.), or they find someplace else to build housing—in cities or states without rent control. When rent control is national there is less housing built throughout the country.

No, Virginia, there is no Santa Claus. Words like *fair rent* or *affordable housing* may bring a warm glow. But they will never build a roof over anybody's head. What these words boil down to is that it would be nice to get housing for what we used to pay. It would also be nice to get automobiles or lamb chops for what we used to pay. All that is different about rent is that it goes up in jumps when the lease expires instead of rising steadily from week to week like groceries.

One of the most deceptive arguments for rent control is that it is only a temporary emergency measure while there is a housing shortage. Sometimes laws against rent increases or condominium conversion are written to apply only when the vacancy rate is below some specified level. What makes such provisions ridiculous is that a temporary housing shortage is made permanent by the law itself. France passed an emergency rent-control law during World War I, and it was still going strong when World War II came along. The "temporary" housing shortage never eased. Hong Kong passed a one-year rent-control law in 1947, and it has been successively extended for more than a quarter of a century.

Housing shortages end after rent control is repealed, not while it is in force. Washington, D.C., and New York City both had housing shortages during World War II under national rent control. After the war national rent control ended, but was replaced by local rent control in New York. In Washington there was no rent control at all. The result? Immediately, there were those "unconscionable" increases in rent we hear so much about, followed by frantic building as "greedy" realtors tried to cash in on the situation. The net result was far more housing, far newer housing, and far cheaper housing in Washington than in New York. That was a generation ago, and political memories are short. Today Washington is into rent control, the very process that has left vast areas of New York full of abandoned and decaying buildings.

In Sweden, rent control was introduced as a temporary wartime measure in 1942. The vacancy rate remained so low that the law was kept in force for more than thirty years. The amount of housing per person declined, despite the building of government housing projects to try to cope with the shortage. Finally, rent control was repealed in 1975. Suddenly, housing increased faster than the population. The vacancy rate rose so high that the government housing projects started running deep in the red and had to be bailed out. Yes, Virginia, there is supply and demand.

Don't Buy a Lemon from Chrysler!

LOS ANGELES HERALD EXAMINER / NOVEMBER 7, 1979

Just when the taxpayers have had it with paying for welfare chiselers, wasteful bureaucrats, and grandiose new programs, along comes the tenth largest industrial corporation in the country with its hand out for federal money. The Chrysler Corporation says it needs $1.5 billion or so to survive. Well, we could all use an extra billion every now and then. Why should the Chrysler Corporation be singled out for this favor?

To add insult to injury, Chrysler claims that it is not "really" asking for a handout, just a "loan guarantee." Coyness by a multi-billion-dollar corporation is a little much. Chrysler has an army of accountants and economists who know perfectly well that the name you call the subsidy makes no real difference economically. All it does is confuse the issue politically, a ploy already used by New York City and Lockheed in their raids on the U.S. Treasury.

If the banks and other professional suppliers of money thought that Chrysler could pay back its loans, why would it be necessary for Uncle Sam to agree to be left holding the bag? Chrysler has already gone deeper in the red than any private business ever has in the history of this country. Even your friendly neighborhood loan company wants to know if you have any visible means of support before letting you have a couple hundred dollars. But if it is the taxpayers' billions, apparently saying "trust me" is enough.

Ironically, Chrysler's inability to stay out of the red is being viewed sympathetically in Washington, at a time when other businesses are being denounced all over the place for making a profit. Both political attitudes show a complete misunderstanding of the economy.

The American economic system is often called a profit system. But that is misleading. Profits are an insignificant part of our national income, and an insignificant part of the price of most products (including gasoline). It is the *opportunity* for profit that is important as an incentive to do things efficiently, and the prospect of losses that forces people to re-examine their decisions. In short, this is a profit *and loss* system. The losses are just as important incentives as the profits. Losses tell the businessman—and his creditors—that he is using up resources that are more valuable than his output. He is not adding value but wasting it.

We do not need a private corporation to waste billions. We already have the federal government to do that. If the government is going to tax people for adding value and subsidize them for wasting it, we should not be surprised when the economy's performance suffers. If producing what the consumer wants becomes less important than manipulating politicians or appeasing noisy "movements," we should not be surprised if businesses start producing more politics and less consumer goods.

The Chrysler Corporation claims that it is losing money because of new government regulations, which make it more expensive to build automobiles. But these regulations apply to other automobile manufacturers—smaller than Chrysler, as well as larger—and they are not drowning in red ink. Actually, government-created costs are only a fraction of Chrysler's losses, or of the subsidy it is seeking. Like many political ploys, it is economic hogwash. It is strange to see liberals being taken in by Chrysler's arguments, which have been exposed and devastated by *Fortune* magazine, hardly an antibusiness publication.

Washington politicians—"liberals" and "conservatives" alike—seem resigned to an inevitable federal bail-out of Chrysler. The only issue seems to be "How much?—and how can it best be disguised?" There are one hundred forty thousand employees of Chrysler, and no one wants to alienate any voters with an election coming up. The U.S. government is like the girl who can't say no.

Dire consequences are always predicted if some special-interest group doesn't get what it wants. Mass unemployment and miscellaneous other disasters are supposed to happen if Chrysler doesn't get its hand in the till. But when people don't buy from Chrysler they are likely to buy from Ford or General Motors, and these companies have to hire workers and buy raw material in order to make cars and trucks. In the short run, a lot of people may be inconvenienced as they transfer to new jobs. But that is always happening in the economy anyway. If a million clerks, waitresses, or secretaries change jobs individually, nobody notices. But a comparable number of changes by workers who are politically organized sends shock waves through Washington. Yet the Chrysler workers have higher pay and better employment benefits than do most of the other workers who are politically ignored. As for the Chrysler owners and managers—if the affluent can't look out for themselves, who can?

How can we complain about spending tax money on welfare mothers or even beach bums who live on food stamps, while handing out $1.5 billion to one of the world's largest corporations? The administration claims that the government will avoid paying unemployment benefits to Chrysler employees who might lose their jobs. That is typical shortsightedness. Unemployment benefits are limited in amount and duration. But once the U.S. Treasury is thrown open to any big corporation in trouble, there are no limits.

The Energy Boondoggle

LOS ANGELES HERALD EXAMINER / JULY 18, 1979

President Carter's speech Sunday night tried to make it sound like zero hour, but it was just amateur hour. The mechanical hand movements, the equally mechanical fist to symbolize strength, the vague clichés about "confidence in the future" and "unity of purpose"—all of these were straight out of some high school debater's speech.

The substance was worse than the style. As with virtually every problem of the past half century, the answer was to create a massive new federal bureaucracy and clamp down new regulations. In the time-tested political formula, all this was washed down with crocodile tears for the poor, who might have to pay higher prices. Since gasoline prices contain more government taxes than oil company profits and filling station profits put together, it would be very easy to reduce the price to the poor—and to everybody else—by getting the government off our backs.

Indeed, we are in all this mess in the first place because the government has imposed price controls on gasoline, and price controls have led to shortages innumerable times over the centuries, whether the product in question was gasoline in modern America or chariots in ancient Rome.

Once the government is into the act, however, they cannot pull back. Things might correct themselves through ordinary economic processes, revealing our political saviors as part of the problem rather than part of the solution. For example, if government controls ended and gasoline prices were determined by supply and demand, like thousands of other prices, what terrible horror would befall us? We might have to pay a quarter more per gallon, but we wouldn't have to reorganize our whole lives around getting into gas lines on odd or even days, or find ourselves up the creek if we ran out of gas at night or on Sunday. And if there were more money to be made by exploring for pertoleum, you can believe the oil companies would go out looking, in order to make a buck (or a buck and a quarter).

That "greed" that we hear denounced so much lately was what kept us well supplied with gasoline for years, at all hours of the day or night. It is what keeps us well supplied with anything else that the government doesn't control.

The fact that people generally supply more of any product at a higher

87

price than at a lower price is one of the first things taught in introductory economics, but politicians seem determined not to learn it. In the political vision of the world, there seems to be a certain amount somehow predestined to be supplied, and the only question is how to price it and regulate it. Because petroleum is an exhaustible resource, politicians can create the impression that either nature or OPEC can be blamed for gasoline lines, or for the "energy crisis" in general.

Actually, all things are finite, just like petroleum, coal, or natural gas. But the amount of petroleum and other energy sources available within the borders of the United States would last for centuries, or even for thousands of years. They will be obsolete before they are exhausted. Naturally, all the oil, coal, gas, etc., is not at the same place, nor the same depth below ground, nor equally easy to process. That means that the amount it pays to locate and extract depends on how much the end products sells for. There is no predestined supply above ground. How much gets taken out of the ground depends on the price.

This is where our political crusaders against "greed" come in. In order to save motorists a few cents a gallon and prevent "windfall profits" by the oil companies, they make it uneconomic to use our own resources, thereby creating the very "dependence on foreign oil" they rant about. In other words, without our own government's controls and red tape holding back American energy production, OPEC wouldn't be able to charge us a bundle for supplying something that we already have under ground.

We don't need a massive government boondoggle to create synthetic fuels. We need to get rid of synthetic politicians and their hokey speeches.

"Automatic Promotion"— at School and Work

THE WASHINGTON STAR / FEBRUARY 24, 1978

One of the bitterest complaints about the public school system has been that it follows a policy of "automatic promotion"—whether the student has learned anything or not. Now that same principle is to be extended past the school age into the job market. People are to be employed automatically, whether they are worth their pay or not. This idea is called by various names, ranging from "full employment" to "government as employer of last resort" to the Humphrey-Hawkins bill.

We have learned the hard way how destructive automatic promotion has been to education in general and, more specifically, to the very children that were supposed to be helped by this apparent generosity. It is ironic that just when this practice is being exposed, criticized, and in some cases reversed, in education, the very same principle of divorcing performance from reward is being touted as the solution to economic problems. It is in fact likely to be even more destructive in the economic sector. As in the case of automatic promotion, the supposed beneficiaries in theory will be the chief victims in practice.

We all know that unemployment is highest among the least skilled, least experienced, and minority workers. Black teenagers have an astronomical unemployment rate. What is not so widely known is that the reduction of the unemployment rate with age is also steepest among blacks. That is, black unemployment rates drop sharply between the teens and the middle to late twenties. This fact is not only important in itself; it is an important clue as to what else is going on in the economic process.

Yet this major fact is constantly ignored by the media and the intelligentsia, preoccupied with finding things with which to indict "society". Although black teenage unemployment is routinely attributed to racism, the black youths whose unemployment rates drop precipitously with age have not changed color as they mature. Moreover, black teenage unemployment 30 years ago was only a fraction of what it is today and no higher than white teenage unemployment at that time—even though racism was certainly not less 30 years ago.

Handicaps by themselves do not produce unemployment. At some pay scale, everyone is employable, and at some much higher pay scale everybody is unemployable. Thirty years ago the minimum wage law had not been changed for a decade, and inflation had practically repealed it. With pay scales free to adjust to the capability or desirability of the worker, the least skilled are just as employable at their wages as the most skilled are at theirs. Blacks had just as high (or higher) labor force participation as whites for every census from 1890 to 1930. It was only after pay scales began to be regulated by minimum wage laws, labor unions, and the like that the least skilled or least favored workers suddenly found themselves "unemployable". Rising teenage unemployment rates, especially among blacks, were among the high costs of such practices.

The rapid decline in black youth unemployment with age suggests that job experience substantially increases their employability, even at wages that made employers reluctant to hire them before. What they acquire is not so much "skills" but such personal habits as punctuality, regularity, discipline and a general shedding of immature traits.

Not all of this happens overnight or without a certain amount of pain on all sides. But it does happen. Performance and reward are closely tied. None of this is peculiar to minority youths, but the principle applies especially where there are special disadvantages.

This whole process is short-circuited when the government steps in as employer of otherwise unemployable youths. Automatic employment in a government program is the direct opposite of employment by a business. No matter what rhetoric the government program uses, it cannot require the same standards of skill or conduct as a business, or those who are unemployable by business would also be unemployable by the government program.

For the program to survive politically, it must put up with employee performance and employee behavior that a private employer could not afford to put up with. If all that this entailed was a loss of efficiency, that might be a minor loss, as government waste goes. What is far more serious—and even tragic—is that young people who need clear and honest signals as to their own performance and the requirements for working with others will be denied both.

Working for an employer who has to hire you is no preparation for working for an employer who doesn't. By tolerating substandard performance and unacceptable behavior, automatic employment (like automatic promotion) merely postpones the day of reckoning and produces more illusions the young person will have to unlearn later if he is ever to be able to cope with the realities of life.

4

THE SOCIAL SCENE

LIFE IS NOT ALL POLITICS AND economics—thank God—and the social world around us is a welcome diversion at times. Sports, the rich, the environment, and the schools are among our many concerns and fascinations. Yet, despite the follies and foibles found in these areas, there is also a pattern to the apparent madness. And it is very similar to the pattern found in politics and economic policy in general—wishful thinking, and resolute blindness to results we do not want to see.

The rich are often a red herring that distracts us from more serious issues. Doomsday doctrines are another distraction that would be funny if the consequences of believing them were not so serious. Environmentalism and education each have their own Alice-in-Wonderland quality, but behind the Mad Hatters and March Hares are some very narrow special interests—and in the background are the future Americans whose fates are in the balance.

Some of these themes are treated lightly, only because it would be a mistake to take self-righteous pomposities seriously. It would in fact be a serious mistake. Understanding why some of these doctrines and movements are ridiculous is a very serious business.

The Rich as a Social Problem

THE WASHINGTON STAR / NOVEMBER 14, 1978

The poor have long been recognized as a social problem. Why not the same recognition for the rich? Once the rich were regarded only as a nuisance or a scandal, but now they seem ready to graduate into a full-fledged Social Problem.

There have always been complaints about the rich. At one time their young people swallowed goldfish or held extravagant debutante balls, and their old people spent fortunes on rare stamps or antique furniture. Little did the rest of us know that those were the good old days. Much of what the rich wanted then—cancelled stamps and old furniture, for example—was not wanted by anyone else, so there was no real social loss. But some people thought the rich should take an interest in more serious things. We never know when to leave well enough alone.

Nowadays the rich are into something called social conscience. It's a status symbol very much like the Stutz Bearcat, and it too uses a lot of gas. The rich are underfoot everywhere, defending every weed or reptile threatened by the construction of a power dam or apartment building. They are providing bail money and lawyer's fees for any well-publicized hoodlum who has the smarts to mix some political rhetoric in with his felonies. The rich are constantly sponsoring "movements," lectures, and rallies to denounce "society," which is apparently to blame for everything from an unhappy sex life to the common cold.

The children of the rich are into the act too. The kind of spoiled rich kids who used to be content with being snotty to the servants now staff terrorist gangs around the world in the interests of "justice" and a Better World. The older or more squeamish rich indulge in terrorism-by-proxy, supporting and romanticizing ghetto gangs to show their concern for the black community.

Then there are the committees, campaigns, and full page ads urging fairness, "understanding," and/or diplomatic recognition of dictators—the right dictators, which is to say, the left dictators. Even at halftime at a football game, the rich kids at Stanford insisted on putting on a pageant honoring a man whose words were orders to a third of the human race, and whose "sayings" were a hot-selling item at the college bookstore. The trendy rich are also on the lookout for aspiring new talent currently in the minor leagues known as "liberation movements." The United States is urged to keep them from being "repressed" by any government that has faults—which is to say, any government. It is appropriate that the leading official spokesman for this viewpoint, Ambassador Andrew Young, is from an affluent background, despite his protective coloration.

Swallowing goldfish has given way to swallowing words. All you have to do is set up an Innovative Community Outreach Genocide Cooperative, with a "chairperson," and some rich people will bankroll it.

It's not only the trendy rich either. Even the average, garden-variety rich are a problem. They are constantly used as a red herring in policy issues concerning the other 99 percent of us. Every hare-brained scheme of rationing or price control is defended as a way of controlling the rich. Every time the taxpayers demand tax reduction, the politicians start talking about tax "reform"—to get at the rich in their tax shelters.

There aren't enough rich people to amount to a hill of beans, as far as taxes are concerned. But the government's big spenders like to get us mad at the rich, instead of mad at them.

With all the problems caused by the rich, what can be done about them? Surely American know-how should be capable of producing enough novelties and status symbols to keep the rich off the streets and out of mischief. If not, perhaps the government could build day-care centers where the rich could receive custodial care and perhaps learn some crafts. With all due respect to our fiscal troubles, it would be a better use of tax money than some others. At the very least, we could recognize them as a social problem. Perhaps recognition is all they want anyway, and the goldfish and the "liberation" movements are just different props used for that same purpose.

The Profits of Doom

THE WASHINGTON STAR / NOVEMBER 22, 1977

For centuries there has been an industry more international than most multinational corporations, more profitable than General Motors, and with more outlets than Sears or Safeway. That industry is the production and distribution of doom.

Doom sells—in religious, political, or ecological versions: in disaster movies, population projections, or I.Q. studies. Universal doomsday— the end of the world—at a specific time and place has been sold to thousands on innumerable occasions. It was almost an annual event at one time. No one's money was ever refunded when the time came and went uneventfully, so there must have been customer satisfaction with the mere foreboding. Why doom is so popular remains a trade secret, like the flavoring in Coca Cola, or Colonel Sanders's herbs and spices.

The profits of doom have been maintained by constantly updating classic models. When science became the new religion, doom began to come equipped with graphs, equations, and computer printouts. The old oracle's trick of sounding specific while being vague took on a statistical dimension. Did you know that more than 40 million Americans each year are gored to death by bulls, pulverized by pile drivers, or otherwise subjected to death, disease, or discomfort? In such statements—which can be found in almost any "movement," social agency, or talk show— the weak stuff at the end supplies the numbers while the strong stuff up front gets the attention.

A rival product called facts is regularly defeated in attempts to compete with this sort of thing. For example, take the population division of the doom industry. The first commercially successful model of overpopulation doom was marketed by Malthus in the late eighteenth century, in the midst of a rising standard of living for the masses which has continued almost uninterruptedly since then. Malthus's overnight success was the beginning of centuries of consumer loyalty to population doom, in spite of any facts.

Back in the 1930s, an underpopulation model was marketed with equal success. Doom was now promised on the basis of declining population growth, which would reduce demand and bring on massive unemployment throughout the Western world. Endorsed by the great English economist J. M. Keynes and by the president of the American Economic Association, this product sold like hotcakes.

94

Within two decades, however, the overpopulation model staged a comeback with the "population bomb" scare. Population growth rates were in fact higher during the underpopulation hysteria than during the overpopulation hysteria, and the latter began after years of continually declining birthrates, which had reached record lows in the United States.

The international version of the population doom model relies on the tried and true merchandising technique of selected examples. For example, there are desperately poor countries with high population density per square mile. Since truth-in-packaging laws do not apply to the doom industry, it is not necessary to note that there are also desperately poor countries with low population density or medium population density, or affluent countries with high, low, and medium population densities. India is often cited by the population division of the doom industry. The fact is that Japan and Western Europe have even higher population densities than India.

Doom marketing is as fascinating as doom production. One technique is the unlimited extrapolation. For example: the temperature has risen fifteen degrees since this morning, and, if this continues unchecked, we will all be burned to a crisp by next Thursday.

With doom, as with any product, the more complex versions tend to develop bugs. President Carter's scientific-looking version of resource-exhaustion doom was going great guns until some analysts fed more realistic assumptions into the computer. Out came the result that we had several centuries' supply of petroleum and thousands of years' supply of natural gas. Fortunately for the president, these were government analysts, who could be simply ordered to change their assumptions to achieve the results that were politically necessary.

Doom sells well by itself or in package deals—with "leadership," for example. Purists will say that this is not true doom, because the pitch is "You are *almost* doomed, but I can save you." Revival-meeting preachers, social reformers, medical quacks, and innumerable sellers of "leadership" of one sort or another have all successfully marketed their respective products this way. Despite the wide variety of complementary products involved, the advertising pitch is basically the same: our salvation requires us to surrender our money and our misused freedom to our leader, who has good uses for both.

Doom goes with everything. It is like ketchup.

What the Sports Snob Misses

THE WASHINGTON STAR / OCTOBER 3, 1978

One of the many ways of showing that you are among the anointed is by looking down your nose at sports. You may not be able to win the Nobel Prize, but at least you can turn off the World Series channel and turn on the "public" television channel, where the latest trendy chatter is being aired. ("Public" television is, of course, noncommercial television that ignores the public, though it does condescend to take the public's tax money to help cover the cost of serving the affluent.)

The intelligentsia take it for granted that sports are "mindless." If they don't understand, there can be nothing to understand. This attitude extends far beyond sports and was once immortalized in a verse about Benjamin Jowett, head of Balliol College at Oxford.

> My name is Benjamin Jowett.
> If it's knowledge, I know it.
> I am the Master of this College,
> What I don't know isn't knowledge.

Even today, it is heresy to believe that there is knowledge, insight, or analysis outside the jurisdictional claims of intellectuals. But sports are just one of many areas where the brain is not a superfluous organ, even if the people using it do not subscribe to the *New York Review of Books*.

If sports were mindless physical feats, we might expect to find its best performances achieved at man's physical peak—around eighteeen years old. But in no major sport is that true.

Nothing looks so simple as a baseball player's running from one base to another before the catcher can throw him out. But the greatest base stealers—Ty Cobb, Maury Wills, and Lou Brock—were all 30 or older before they had their record-breaking seasons. Accumulated expertise in "reading" pitchers and analyzing game situations apparently offset whatever loss of foot speed occurred with aging. Certainly no one can believe that Lou Brock was running faster at age 35, when he broke the base-stealing record, than he was at age 22, when he entered the major leagues.

In professional football, it is seldom that a rookie quarterback becomes a star, however spectacular he may have been in college and however magnificent he later becomes as a pro. Pro football quarter-

96

backs are likely to be older at their peaks than mathematicians are at theirs.

No one who saw Suger Ray Robinson outbox bigger, stronger, or younger men can believe that sports lack intelligence and subtlety just because they are expressed physically. The many victories of Dick Weber in bowling and Gary Player in golf over bigger and brawnier opponents also give the lie to the notion that it is all muscle and sweat.

Some critics point out that nothing is happening most of the time in a baseball game or a football game. The same is true of chess. The fact that sports fans are often at a pitch of excitement while nothing is happening on the field suggests that something is happening in their minds. Who was ever bored while Joe DiMaggio slowly walked toward the plate to face Bob Feller with the bases loaded? Possibilities, tactics, and alternatives are as much a part of sports as the actual course of events that materializes before your eyes.

Sports have a number of advantages over some activities with more intellectual pretensions. Perhaps the most important is that sports are for real. When Roger Staubach fades back to pass in the closing seconds with the game in the balance, you know damned well he wants to connect with someone in the end zone. What he is supposed to do, and what he looks like he is doing, is in fact what he is doing. Compare that with the pretensions of "experts" spouting off on things on which there can be no expertise, or a politician explaining away his blunders, or even the Supreme Court claiming to "interpret" the Constitution while they impose their own policy preferences.

If sports are an escape, they are an escape from phoniness. Part of the appeal of sports is that you can believe in it, at a time when you cannot believe in presidents, the courts, or the so-called United Nations.

Educational Draftees

LOS ANGELES HERALD EXAMINER / SEPTEMBER 12, 1979

Millions of young people are starting the annual trek back to schools ranging from kindergarten to college and postgraduate studies. For many, it is a golden opportunity. For others, they and the taxpayers might well ask, "Is this trip necessary?"

There has developed a tendency to speak piously of education as if it had an aura around it—something not to be defiled with facts or common sense. But great numbers of recipients of educational "opportunity" are in school not because they want to be, but because they have to be. They are part of a vast army of scholastic draftees, going to school with the attitudes of draftees. Much of the vandalism, falling standards, and even violence that erupts at all levels of school are a natural consequence of keeping millions of people in a place where they fundamentally don't want to be.

Everyone recognizes the need for literacy and other educational basics. But compulsory-attendance laws have been applied to keep youths in school long past the time necessary to learn these things. Despite much pious rhetoric about the benefits to the youngsters, the cold fact is that many youths are simply being warehoused in schools until the powers that be find it convenient to let them enter the labor force.

Labor union lobbyists have long spearheaded efforts to apply the compulsory attendance laws to successively older children. The present draftee army in the schools did not just happen. The same union lobbyists have also cut off young people's options with so-called child labor laws preventing them from working. The propaganda for such laws conjures up images of ten-year-olds working in the coal mines or around dangerous factory machinery. The reality today is that such laws prevent a man-sized teenager from carrying a piece of paper in an air-conditioned office. A more grim effect of such laws is that young people who find school (or home) intolerable and go off on their own find few ways to stay alive except thievery or prostitution.

In many ways school children are not beneficiaries but pawns—creating jobs for teachers and empires for layers of administrators ranging all the way up to the Department of Health, Education, and Welfare. Children are merely the raw material that keeps this vast machinery turning for the benefit of others.

Even at the college level, many students are not there because they want to be, but because they feel they have to be. College degrees are increasingly required for jobs which involve no erudition or special skills. Diplomas are a way of separating job applicants into the sheep and the goats—a useful convenience for employers, but a costly process for taxpayers and a waste of precious years when many young adults would be happier doing something else. The psychiatric problems and suicides among college students are part of the hidden costs of insisting that everyone accumulate as many diplomas as possible.

If this was all just a misplaced zeal for learning, it might be excusable. But actual learning has been sacrificed in the rush to fill classrooms with warm bodies. Test scores have been falling all over the country, from Ivy League colleges to ghetto high schools. The rising grades that have accompanied falling performances are perfectly understandable once we realize that this is a public relations or political operation, not education. The name of the game is not learning, but body count, appropriations, jobs, and empires.

Some rethinking is long overdue on the scope of compulsory-attendance laws and the whole monopolistic nature of the public schools. We don't trust monopoly in other parts of our society. The performance of our two biggest monopolies—the post office and the public schools—suggests that our distrust is wellfounded.

Environmentalists and Ego Trips

THE WASHINGTON STAR / DECEMBER 5, 1978

The Sierra Club arranges many kinds of trips, but its specialty is the ego trip. To the rest of us, Sierra Clubbers and other woodsy types may be much like tennis players, bowling leagues, or music groups. They are just doing their own thing. In their own eyes, though, they are not just another special interest. They are the guardians of what they call "the environment" or "the ecology" or even "the ecosystem."

Who appointed them guardians? God? The Constitution? Or has there been some election, referendum, plebiscite, contract, proxy vote, coronation, or other procedure investing them with the right to override other people's preferences in favor of their own?

Rules and institutions exist precisely because people disagree, and there must be mechanisms for weighing and accommodating different interests. But the "commitment" approach to public policy wants no part of that.

One way is to put decisions in the hands of nonelected commissions, boards, and advisory groups. Their mere power of delay can run up construction costs by millions of dollars, making it economically unfeasible to build power plants, apartment buildings, or even bicycle paths that the appointees don't want built. Studies show that the required "environmental impact" reports do not in fact make valid predictions about what impacts will be on the environment.

Even the most laissez-faire economists agree that air and water pollution require government action. It is one thing to take direct action against pollution. It is something else to use pollution dangers as the entering wedge for a massive expansion of a fanatic minority's political power.

The "environmentalist" conception is of a static balance in nature, when in fact environments have been changing for untold millions of years. Plants, animals, and whole patterns of interrelationship among them have come and gone thousands of times during the eons of evolution. Now suddenly by government fiat, the current organisms and their particular balance are to be preserved forever as *the* environment. If evolution had been called to a halt like this in the age of the dinosaurs, human beings would never have come into existence.

Under pressure from "environmentalists," the government has evicted people from their homes to expand national parks, and destroyed the jobs of loggers, fishermen, and others. It has taken over 99 percent of the land in Alaska to let recreation interests use, leaving the other 1 percent for everyone else. Every weed or reptile that goes on the "endangered species" list can hold up any construction, however urgently needed.

Sometimes the government puts its power on the side of certain groups, on the assumption that those groups have some special disadvantage. Far from being disadvantaged, Sierra Clubbers are overwhelmingly high-income professionals. Faded jeans and all, they are monied people using the government to take things from others to satisfy a special-interest group.

The government may pander to their illusion of simplicity in the wilds, but an elaborate organization of everything from medical and food supplies to electronic communication to forest rangers, helicopter rescue teams, and a whole bureaucracy of the National Park Service hovers in the background while the doctors and engineers troop about in the woods pretending to be primitive. Meanwhile, back in Washington, their lobbyists work full time on Congress to give them more of an outdoor playground at other people's expense.

There is nothing wrong with wanting outdoor recreation or even indulging in illusions—at your own expense. When you do it by force, using the power of government, that is something else. And when nonelected zoning boards and coastal commissions forbid the construction of apartment buildings that would give a view of the ocean to the moderate-income many in order to reserve it for the affluent few, then "ecosystem" rhetoric has become a camouflage for an undemocratic ego system.

Hype versus Higher Education

LOS ANGELES HERALD EXAMINER / JANUARY 9, 1980

Colleges and universities are big business. Some are virtual cities in themselves, with populations of 30,000 to 50,000. There are about five times as many college faculty members as there are employees of the Chrysler Corporation. And the academics have been bailed out by the federal government much longer.

Colleges share in the pious sanctity that goes with being a "nonprofit" organization. Many businesses make smaller profits than the salary of a university president, much less the millions that are handed out in grants on a typical university campus. But a profit is without honor, while well-paid academics are portrayed as dedicated and selfless.

When a business advertises, it pays thousands of dollars for a page in a newspaper or magazine, and hundreds of thousands for a commercial on television. But college profs and presidents get free time and free space to plug their product in interviews, columns, or "public service" announcements. The reader or viewer isn't even warned that it is advertising. It is treated as news—and of a particularly noble kind.

Big-time college football on television usually carries a halftime announcement advertising the academic virtues of the schools that are playing. Truth-in-advertising laws must not apply to these sentimental vignettes. They depict a kind of intellectual Olympus, even when the institution is little more than a football team with a campus attached.

Like any other business with millions of dollars to protect, colleges and universities are always anxious about the market for their product. Population statistics show that there are going to be fewer college-age people in the next decade. Academia can either gracefully accept declining revenues (not bloody likely) or hype up the advertising to drum up more business. We can look forward to a lot of new hype.

Some colleges are already using commercial advertising firms to design their catalogues and even their curriculums. Never mind what courses are needed to educate. They want courses that will sell. Even in those places that have not openly gone that far in hype, the trend is to de-emphasize hard stuff like math or boring stuff like history or logic. What is promoted is stuff fresh out of the headlines—"innovative" education, as it is called. Courses (or whole departments) are being created in women's liberation, environmentalism, or Third World–ism.

Some colleges boast of having no particular course requirements

102

whatsoever for graduation. Any course you don't like, you don't take. You don't have to choose any existing major and meet its requirements. You can create your own individual major and study whatever you feel like to get a degree in it. Never has it been easier to graduate from college as a complete ignoramus.

Ironically, many of the same people who advocate economic controls, to restrict what adults can do with their own money, are in favor of allowing adolescents wider scope in what they can do with the taxpayers' money. More and more of higher education is supported by the taxpayers. Many private colleges and universities are going out of business, while state colleges and universities are expanding. In addition, even private institutions are heavily subsidized by the federal government. Doing your own thing is not just your own business when it is done with someone else's money.

It is not just the competition for existing students that is undermining academic standards. There is also a constant effort to pull people onto campus who would not ordinarily be there. Colleges are pictured as the answer to all sorts of problems—psychological, financial, or social. Courses are created in everything from horseback riding to real estate to soap operas. The question is not whether these are worthy activities. The question is why the taxpayer should have to pay the bill for them. Another question is whether a college or university should have its own specific role, or just be a shopping mall where everything imaginable can be found.

Perhaps the most cynical aspect of the search for new customers is the drive to get more minority youngsters on campus, at places where the existing minority students are flunking out in droves. The drive to get more warm bodies that the college administration can report to the feds—in order to keep government money coming in—is depicted as a great humanitarian or social undertaking. But there is little humanitarianism in having a youngster's hopes raised unrealistically, then wasting two or three years of his life as he struggles to meet standards for which he lacks preparation, and finally booting him out after he has served his statistical purpose. It is not uncommon for more than half the minority students at a college to leave with no degree.

The issue is not whether colleges and universities serve a useful purpose. The issue is whether they should continue to receive blank checks. When they are just looking out for number one, it is time for the taxpayer to start doing the same.

Those Phony Environmentalists

LOS ANGELES HERALD EXAMINER / MARCH 23, 1979

Few things are more fascinating than the arguments of the rich as they explain why the government should help them in their battles with the poor. The story line is simple: Land and water are limited, like everything else. Everybody wants more, but there is more "everybody" than there is "more." Obviously, there is going to have to be somebody left on the outside looking in. Those who are on the inside looking out want to make sure they keep their spots. It is the simplicity of great art, with ingenious touches, like keeping a main character always offstage as in *Rebecca* or *Duffy's Tavern*, where we never saw Rebecca or Duffy.

Low and moderate income people are cast in the offstage villain's role of someone who wants to foreclose on the old homestead held by the affluent heroes. This much of the drama is true to life. The poor do foreclose on the rich, through the marketplace, because *the poor have more money*. There are infinitely more of them, and real estate dealers and developers would rather get $10 million from 10,000 people than get $1 million from one millionaire.

In the natural course of economic events, the non-rich would end up taking more and more land and shore away from the rich. Spectacular homes with spectacular views would be replaced by mundane apartment buildings with only moderately pleasant vistas. A doctor or movie mogul who can now walk the beach in front of his house in splendid isolation would be replaced by whole families of ordinary grubby mortals seeking a respite from the asphalt and an occasional view of the sunset.

The climax of the story is when the affluent heroes are rescued by the government. In the old days, this used to be the cavalry, but nowadays it is more likely to be the zoning board or the coastal commission. They decree that the land cannot be used in ways that would make it accessible to the many, but only in ways accessible to the few. Legal phrasing is of course more elaborate and indirect than this, but that is what it all boils down to. This is called "preserving the environment" (applause) from those who would "misuse" it (boos).

Although the villains, whose use is defined as *misuse*, are kept offstage, there must be someone on stage to boo and hiss. The favorite in this role is the old stage banker who used to threaten the sanctity of the (mortgaged) home or the virtue of the young daughter therein, or both.

Now it is the land that is being threatened with what used to be called "a fate worse than death."

Why the banker would want the daughter would be easy to see (if the right actress were cast in the role), but why the developer would want the land is not nearly so obvious. Actually, he does not want the land at all. He wants to sell it or rent it to those offstage villains, the nonaffluent. The battle against the developer is a sham battle, fought with him only because the whole drama would be ruined by a cast of thousands on stage.

The offstage villains are sometimes balanced with offstage heroes—"posterity," in whose name the climactic battle is fought. It is not clear just when posterity elected our affluent heroes as their spokesmen; but then, drama cannot let itself get bogged down in details.

"Educators" Treat Parents Like Children

LOS ANGELES HERALD EXAMINER / NOVEMBER 14, 1979

In a country founded on freedom of choice, it is amazing how many battles still have to be fought over that issue. The big battle now shaping up is over vouchers that would enable parents to send their children to whatever school they choose.

Everybody is for freedom in the abstract. It is only when you get to freedom in the concrete that you run into opposition. To many of the Olympians in our universities, government, and courts, concrete free choice by ordinary grubby mortals is a scary, if not repulsive, idea. It is especially likely to be repulsive as regards children, for whom the Olympians have their own grand designs.

All sorts of bogeymen are brought out of the closet to scare us away from the idea of parental free choice. One bogeyman is that parents don't really understand education and would make terrible choices. Considering the many disasters in the public schools created by "experts" over the past ten or twenty years, it is hard to imagine how parents could do worse.

As the cost per pupil has soared, the students' test scores have plummeted. As the number of students has gone down, the number of administrators has gone up. As the "sex education" fad spread, under the guise of reducing venereal disease and teenage pregnancy, venereal disease and teenage pregnancy have reached new heights. As rules and discipline have been relaxed or eliminated to make children happier, teenage suicide has also reached new heights.

The education "experts" have failed at virtually everything they have put their hands to. Johnny not only can't read, he can't think. But he can smoke pot and get girls pregnant—and repeat sociological excuses for his behavior. The education experts' only success has been at snowing the public—and even that is coming to an end, as voters have started turning down school bond issues around the country.

The claim that parents don't really understand education is especially ironic coming from education officials who dress up every simple idea in the most elaborate jargon. Even a simple word like *competence* has to be stretched out an extra syllable into *competency*. Empty barrels make the most noise—and use the longest words.

A parent doesn't have to be an expert on the inner workings of schools to be able to choose one that produces good results for his or her child.

The real problem for the education establishment is precisely that parents *can* judge end results. Those schools or teachers or administrators who cannot produce results would be out of business if the parents had freedom of choice. No longer would smooth and lofty excuses be enough.

Sometimes the education bureaucrats are willing to concede that some parents can make choices. But they claim that this is not true of parents who are less educated, poor, or black. It is precisely the children of these kinds of parents who get the worst education today, from the very education experts who claim to want to protect them from parental free choice.

It has been a long time since poor or minority parents have been able to exercise free choice. The education establishment has been in tight control for generations, with compulsory-attendance laws and civil service rules that make it nearly impossible to fire a teacher. What happened before the education establishment got this power? Did poor or minority parents shirk their responsibility?

The first compulsory-attendance law took effect in 1852. But the great majority of Americans were already literate by then. These were people much poorer than we are today, and many of them lived in rural isolation, miles from the nearest school. Parents obviously had some concern for educating their children, even without Big Brother.

What of blacks? In the 1850s, there were about half a million free blacks. They were even poorer than the whites, and they were not permitted to attend public school in the North or South. In some parts of the South, they were forbidden to attend any school, even privately, at their own expense. As late as 1855, a black man was publicly whipped in the nation's capitol for conducting an unauthorized school for black children.

You might think that no blacks could get an education under these circumstances. But you would be wrong. Three out of five free blacks were found to be literate in the 1850 census. In the big cities the proportion was higher. More than 90 percent of the free blacks were literate in some cities, even in states where schools for blacks were outlawed. "Underground" schools for free blacks existed all over the South. Rural isolation kept more free blacks illiterate than the law did.

Hard to imagine blacks going to private schools? That was the only kind of schooling most ever received until well after the Civil War. It was 1918 before there were as many black youngsters in public high schools as in private high schools. Today a majority of blacks polled are in favor of vouchers. Naturally, the paternalists who play Big Brother to blacks do not want them to have this free choice.

The public school establishment is by no means as indispensable as they would have us believe. Where they have something good to offer, let them offer it. But don't let them continue to cram their product down people's throats. It doesn't make sense to deny parents a choice. And it is inexcusable when the real victims are children.

5

COURTS AND THE LAW

LAW IS WHAT MAKES CIVILIZED society possible. Any tribal chief can give orders and punish those who don't obey. But what makes law different is that we live under rules, and not under the whims of despots.

The idea of "a government of laws and not of men" is the foundation of American democracy. Not even the president of the United States could openly defy this principle without paying a high price—and in the case of Richard Nixon, many Americans wanted him to pay a still higher price. But whatever the appropriate punishment, the principle is uncontested: no one is above the law.

The sacredness of the law has been used, however, to suggest a sanctity of judges. Over the past generation, judges have played larger and larger roles in making decisions that once were made by elected officials, private individuals, or voluntary organizations. Judges have in fact come very close to assuming the kinds of sweeping powers once exercised by tribal chiefs. The growing powers of courts have come to threaten the very concept of law. Yet any criticism of judges is regarded as undermining the law. This attitude leaves judges free to continue undermining the law themselves.

The police, whose job it is to enforce the law, have increasingly discovered that this is no simple matter, because what is called the law so often boils down lately to what a majority of appellate judges happen to think. Judges repeatedly change the very meaning of a crime, as well as how a criminal may or may not be captured or jailed. In safety and comfort, judges may take weeks or months to second-guess a decision that a policemen had one second to make, at the peril of his life. Politicians and journalists often do the same, with similar safety, comfort, and leisure.

The genuine misdeeds of some policemen are a serious concern. Such policemen are in many ways similar to judges who act as if what they personally want to do *is* the law. Yet these are seldom recognized as twin dangers. Supporters of judges think the policemen are dangerous. And supporters of the police think that judges are dangerous.

Both are dangerous when they fail to respect the very law they are sworn to uphold. In our time it has become more fashionable to overlook it when judges twist the law for "good" purposes. But the whole point of law is that we are not to be ruled by fashions or whims or arbitrary orders. The essays that follow try to make this point in a variety of ways and settings.

Judges versus the Law

LOS ANGELES HERALD EXAMINER / OCTOBER 24, 1979

Many decisions that used to be all in the family are now all in the courtroom. Recently, parents who wanted to spare their dying child the pain of chemotherapy were hit by a court order by a judge who thought that he knew better. They had to flee the country to avoid tormenting their child with treatments that they saw as futile.

Another judge has sternly separated a small child from the only parents he knew—foster parents who wanted to adopt him. They are white and the child is black, and "experts" told the judge that there could be problems for a child growing up in an interracial home. Apparently life will be a bowl of cherries for him in an orphanage.

The point is not simply that judges have been wrong. Anyone who sits down and honestly adds up the times he has been wrong will find the experience humbling, if not humiliating. The problem is that judges' mistakes are hard to correct. Moreover, courts are increasingly intruding into new areas where other people know much more about the situation than any judge could possibly know. Relying on "expert" testimony is often an exercise in self-delusion. There are no experts on many issues. Nowhere is it written in the stars that there is an expert for every subject. Certainly there are lots of people ready to sound off for a fee, but that is something else.

Worst of all, the experience of people who actually suffer the consequences of court decisions is often dismissed as "public clamor". It doesn't carry anywhere near as much weight as the speculations of theorists.

Judges have expanded their role tremendously over the past generation. They prescribe the wattage of light bulbs in a prison. They entangle people in marriage laws when the people have been living together precisely to avoid that. They even tell legislatures to pass certain tax laws. Judges no longer apply the law. They make the law. If Congress passes a law they don't like, the judges reinterpret it out of existence. Anyone who reads the Civil Rights Act of 1964 will never understand how quotas can be legal today.

Many supporters of judicial activism say that is how it should be. They see the role of judges as setting values rather than applying rules. Their model was Chief Justice Earl Warren, who would interrupt a lawyer's argument to demand, "But is it *right*? Is it *good*?"

Of course the only reason for bothering to write down laws in the first place is that different people have different ideas of what is right or good. A law says what we have decided to do, so that life can go on regardless of our differences. If motorists had to decide at every intersection whether it was right or good for one car to cross before another, it would be nearly impossible for anyone to get anywhere safely. Instead, traffic lights arbitrarily let the traffiic in one direction go first, whether it is more deserving or not. Long ago, Supreme Court Justice Robert H. Jackson reminded his colleagues that the Constitution of the United States is not a suicide pact. It was something that people were meant to live with—not something to destroy them by being carried to ever more extreme lengths by judges.

The Constitution said that we have the right to our lawyer's advice when we are on trial. The judges stretched that to mean that the taxpayers have to pay for the lawyer for many cases. Then they stretched it again to mean that a court-appointed lawyer had to raise every conceivable issue, however unfounded, or the defendant had been deprived of his constitutional rights. Moreover, the defendant had the right to demand to be his own lawyer. If the request was denied, he could appeal the denial. If the request was granted and he lost the case, he could appeal on grounds of lack of competent counsel. While this whole game was going on with newly created rules, thousands of violent criminals would be walking the streets, awaiting trial in an already overcrowded court system.

The judges have brought us dangerously close to the point where the Constitution is being converted into a suicide pact. We would not be the first society to strangle itself with its own red tape. The Roman empire and the great Chinese dynasties were both helped along the road to destruction by the growth of excessive rules and regulations.

At one time there was a philosophy called judicial restraint, which kept judges from carrying every principle as far as it could possibly be stretched. Nowadays, judicial restraint is out of fashion. For many people, that is worse than being wrong.

If judges will not restrain themselves, the choice is to have them restrained by others or to let them wreak all the havoc they can. Judges who act like little tin gods can be removed from the bench. If present laws do not permit this, those laws can be amended. The real obstacle is not so much the existing law as the existing attitude. As long as we are too awed by judges to impeach them for overstepping their authority, they will misuse their power, as all sorts of other human beings have misused theirs. Respect for the law is not a blank check for judges. Respect for the law means that even judges are not above it.

112

Crime and Punishment

LOS ANGELES HERALD EXAMINER / OCTOBER 10, 1979

Controversy has been raging for a long time between those who favor a "soft" approach and those who favor a "hard" approach to punishing criminals. But much of what actually happens in the legal system combines the worst features of both approaches.

The basic problem is that the law hands out penalties in installments. The first installment is likely to be turning the criminal loose after some sociological mumbo jumbo about "rehabilitation" or (the other magic word) "community" release. The young offender, especialy, is likely to get the idea that the law is a paper tiger that can be defied and mocked. As he continues down the same road, the law slowly begins to act, sometimes only after many arrests and convictions.

But just as the law is slow to start punishing, it is slow to stop. Installments keep coming long after the criminal has stopped raising hell and may be trying to settle down to raise a family. A prison record dogs him wherever he goes, cutting off his opportunities, making him a social pariah and generally painting him into a corner. Would it not have been more humane, as well as more effective, to have given the young offender a quick rap across the knuckles, to let him know the law means business?

The ever more elaborate "rights" and "due process" which encircle the criminal have been criticized as unfair to the victim or to society. They may also be unfair to the criminal, especially the young offender who is repeatedly misled into believing that the law has no real teeth. By the time those teeth are finally sunk into him, it may be too late for him and too late for his victims.

The soft-liners and the hard-liners both contribute to this tragic situation. The soft-liners dress up their indecision and cop-outs as deeper insight into the social causes of crime. Being poor, under-privileged, and discriminated against are supposed to cause crime. But in the midst of the worst depression in history, people in the tenements of Harlem could go sleep out in the park on hot summer nights. Today nobody would dare do that, even in affluent and overprivileged neighborhoods. Armed guards in public schools are another phenomenon of our affluent—and vacillating—times.

The hard-liners contribute to the problem by refusing to do anything about impossible prison conditions. Even a judge who has both feet on

PINK AND BROWN PEOPLE

the ground and has the guts to enforce the law is going to hesitate to send a young man with a minor offense to an overcrowded prison snakepit, where he is likely to be terrorized and gang-raped.

It will cost hard cash to maintain enough prison capacity to eliminate overcrowding and the breakdown of internal prison discipline that goes with it. It will cost tax dollars to hire the quantity and quality of guards needed to put the prison population under control of the authorities instead of under the prison terrorists.

This isn't coddling criminals. This is protecting society. At the very least, it means giving the judge a place where he can send a young offender for a minor punishment rather than a dehumanizing trauma. Right now, there is nothing much in between letting him go scot-free and letting him be devastated as a human being.

Politicians like to spend money on constituents who will vote for them, or on groups toward whom the general public feels sympathetic. No politician wants to champion the cause of more money for jailbirds. The public itself has to demand enough prison facilities and prison personnel to allow a conscientious judge to let criminals know from the outset that the law means business.

Money is absolutely necessary, but money alone will not do it. The whole criminal justice area needs to be cleansed of the excuse-mongers, faddists, sentimentalists, and assorted zanies and hustlers who infest the system. Enormous power has been put into the hands of anonymous little cliques who can parole murderers or leave convicted drug-pushers at large in "rehabilitation" programs or put hoodlums back on the street in "community" organizations.

The people to whom such powers have been delegated are usually elected by nobody, accountable to nobody, and meet no qualifications standard other than talking the rest of us into putting them on parole boards or funding their high-sounding programs. If "prison reform" means continuing to subsidize this crowd, it has no chance. It ought to mean adequate facilities to house prisoners and protect the public.

Are Cops' Lives Cheap?

LOS ANGELES HERALD EXAMINER / JUNE 20, 1979

Asking someone to lay down his life is no small thing, no matter what kind of uniform he wears—whether a policeman, fireman, or soldier. Underneath that uniform is a flesh-and-blood human being, who wants to see the sunshine tomorrow just as much as you or I. Somewhere in the background are others whose lives would never be the same without him.

From time to time some policeman finds himself in a situation where life or death hangs on his decision. He can pull his gun to defend himself or the public, or he can take a chance that he can handle a dangerous situation without it—and perhaps pay with his life if he is wrong. Often he has no more than a second or two to make up his mind. Others with much more leisure and safety can later take weeks or months to second-guess him if he shoots, pointing out wisely how they think it should have been handled. Perhaps if the policeman had had a few weeks or months to think about it, he might have handled it differently too.

Every situation is different, and every policeman is different. That is going to be true as long as police departments are staffed by human beings. Neither the police department nor the public should tolerate someone who is trigger-happy. But neither should we be stampeded by those critics for whom indignation is a way of life or who weigh policemen's lives very lightly in the balance.

Part of the problem are the hopelessly unrealistic expectations of what a cop can know or do. In the movies or on television, the hero can shoot the villain in his left wrist at 50 yards, making him drop his gun, after beating him to the draw in a split second. In a real life-and-death situation, you would be lucky to hit anyone anywhere with a revolver shot at 20 yards. What part of the anatomy the bullet would land in, if it hits at all, is anybody's guess. The distinction between shooting and "shooting to kill" is fine in theory, but sometimes it has no realistic meaning in practice.

It is a messy, ugly, chancy situation. Those of us who are privileged not to have to face it can at least have the decency not to make unrealistic demands on those who do.

Sometimes the argument is made, "Surely two big, strong policemen could have arrested him without shooting him." All that seems to matter to people who talk this way is whether the criminal finally ends up behind bars. How many policemen or members of the public he injures or kills before they subdue him doesn't seem to matter. Someone armed with a knife is a potential killer, and anyone killed by a knife is just as dead as if they had been blasted by a cannon. It isn't just a game where all that matters is who wins at the end. It is also a question of how much blood gets shed along the way—and whose blood.

The same shortsightedness is shown by those who are quick to cry "overreaction" whenever a large contingent of police is sent to put down a disturbance. A smaller number of policemen might have been able to "win" in a battle, but a large number can reduce the possibility of a battle in the first place. The police, the public, and even those creating the disturbance may end up better off when an obviously overwhelming force of policemen shows up.

The great, unspoken assumption underlying many of the criticisms is that a policeman's life should be risked to avoid risking someone else's life—even a criminal's life. Risking his life is supposed to be part of his job, just like wearing the uniform. But because he has agreed to put his life on the line to protect ours does not mean we should multiply the risks of the job. We certainly don't pay him anything like the pay of a test pilot or a stunt man.

One of the current battlegrounds in cities around the country is the issue of a civilian review board to look at charges of police brutality or excessive force. Those who argue that no organization should be its own judge and jury certainly have a point in principle. But the critics' own irresponsibility in the charges and demands on policemen have made this prospect something to be questioned, not only by the police but by the general public.

A feeling that nobody else knows or cares what they are up against will cause men to stick together and protect even the bad apples among them. If we want more reasonable procedures for reviewing police behavior in emergencies, we have to have more reasonable expectations—including an understanding that there are people under those uniforms. And that their lives are not cheap.

Lawlessness in the Law

LOS ANGELES HERALD EXAMINER / FEBRUARY 20, 1980

The past generation has seen a bitter battle over the law—between people who advocate very similar principles. On one side are the law-and-order types who want to "unleash" the police. On the other side are those who support judges' keeping a tight control on police—and on schools, businesses, and all sorts of other institutions. They want to "unleash" the judges.

Those who want the police turned loose to do their job in their own way seem to envisage someone like Kojak on television or Sheriff Buford Pusser in the *Walking Tall* movies. These lawmen lean on the the punks and rough up the bad guys as they see fit, without worrying about the Constitution. They do whatever they think is "right".

The liberals are horrified at letting lawmen be lawless. But their heroes are people like Chief Justice Earl Warren, who never let the Constitution stand in his way when it came to doing good, as he saw it. Warren is fondly remembered as the man who interrupted lawyers' arguments in the Supreme Court to ask, "But is it *right*? Is it *good*?"

However offensive the comparison may be to both sides, Earl Warren and Buford Pusser were birds of a feather. Both were concerned with "results" and were not about to let the written law cramp their style. Both have many admirers and many imitators.

There are policemen who make themselves judge and jury and hand out their own brand of punishment—especially when their victims are poor, ill-educated, and unable to defend their rights. Some consider it their job to offset the leniency of the courts. In one southern town, the saying among the police is, "You may beat the rap, but you won't beat the ride." They clobber you in the police car on the way to the station.

Some judges also see the issue as a tug-of-war between the courts and the cops. And they are determined to show the police who is boss, even at the expense of the public's safety. One such judge in New York is known as Turn-'em-Loose Bruce. There are many other judges whom that title would fit, even if it didn't rhyme. Whenever a vicious criminal is convicted in California, we have to hold our breath to see if Rose Bird and Company can twist the law beyond recognition in order to turn him loose.

The whole idea of law is that we will operate with rules. Nobody is supposed to throw his weight around just because he has the power,

117

whether he wears a blue uniform or a black robe. Everyone knows this. The problem is that too many people are ready to wink at it—if it is done by those on their side.

Any attempt to control the lawlessness committed by officials of the law will bring out their respective partisans, screaming bloody murder. Try suggesting that we tighten the controls on judges' discretion, or more readily impeach judges who overstep the bounds. Outraged liberals will denounce this as an attack on the law and an attempt to bring politics into it. Suggest that the police are not the ones to investigate the police and you will hear the same words and music on the other side.

Editorialists periodically express shock and indignation that some policemen make distinctions in their treatment of different classes of citizens. But many of those same editorialists supported Rose Bird's election after she enumerated the classes of people for whom the law should show special concern. Apparently it was just a question of whose ox was gored, rather than a principle of equal protection of the law.

Certainly the law is too important to be tinkered with every time someone has a bright idea. But the sanctity of the law implies no sanctity of policemen or judges. Both may need to be reminded of that from time to time, by seeing some of their erring colleagues thrown out into the street to find out what it is like to be an ordinary mortal again.

The Bird

LOS ANGELES HERALD EXAMINER / JUNE 27, 1979

It is the year 2,000. Spotlights are focused on a stage, where the master of ceremonies, in elegant tuxedo, is addressing the audience. "Gentle persons, tonight we are making the annual Rose Bird award, for the outstanding judge of the year." A woman in a unisex pantsuit walks over and hands him three envelopes.

"Our first nominee is Judge Balch. He issued a court order to demolish all churches in Washington, D.C., and in all 50 state capitals, as violations of the constitutional separation of church and state."

Applause.

"Our second nominee is Judge Henley, the first judge to order the busing of school children across the ocean."

A standing ovation.

"Our final nominee is Judge Gurk. He freed a man convicted of 25 murders when he noticed that the arresting policeman's socks did not match. This made the policeman out of uniform, invalidating the arrest and making the confession to the 25 murders inadmissible in court."

Wild applause and cries of "Bravo!"

"Who will win, gentle persons? Who will receive the coveted statue of Chief Justice Rose Bird, who pioneered the legal trends we are honoring tonight? Who will receive this little statue we call the Bird? Which of these judges deserves to get the Bird? The envelope, please." A man in a chartreuse shirt and flamingo-pink slacks bounces on stage and hands him the envelope.

"And the winner is—Chief Justice Mortimer Gurk of the U.S. Supreme Court!"

A spotlight picks out the chief justice, standing at the back of the audience in his long black robe. As he starts down the aisle amid tumultuous applause, the band plays "Hail to the Chief."

As he walks up on stage, the chief justice is obviously emotionally moved, and dabs at his eyes with a handkerchief. "Thank you so much, gentle persons. I want to thank all those who have helped me get here tonight—my parents, my psychiatrist, and above all, my professors in law school."

The chief justice pauses to pull himself together. Then, with a far-off look of nostalgia, he begins to reminisce.

"I can still remember when I was a first-year law student. Before my

119

professors showed me the way, how little I knew of the law! How little I knew of how to interpret our dynamic and innovative Constitution!

"On the first day of class, kindly old Professor Tribe asked me what was the purpose of law. I was so ignorant, I said, 'To protect the public.' "

Gasps from the audience.

"Yes, I know it is hard to believe. But some of you old-timers may remember when people still thought that way! I was a victim of society and the times. Back in those days, there were so many injustices. Toilets still had signs on them saying 'men' and 'women'. People still thought Congress and state legislatures should make the law, instead of the courts." Some younger members of the audience look at each other in amazement.

"But my law professors cured me of all that. They taught me the true meaning of equality under the Constitution—that people must be treated equally, whether they are guilty or innocent, criminals or policemen, competent or incompetent."

Another standing ovation.

The master of ceremonies hands him the little statue of Rose Bird. Again, Gurk is choked with emotion. "This little statue means so much to me! It symbolizes everything we aspire to! It is as inspiring to me as the giant Statue of Judicial Supremacy in New York Harbor (formerly the Statue of Liberty)."

"You certainly deserve it, sir."

"I shall try to be worthy of it. There are still many legal battles remaining to be fought. Even now the Supreme Court has momentous cases pending. The American Civil Liberties Union wants to have police departments abolished. Ralph Nader wants business declared unconstitutional.

"Since I am among friends, I can tell you that these cases have already been decided, but the results won't be released until after the election."

After a round of handshakes on stage, Chief Justice Gurk heads back down the aisle, clutching his statue of Rose Bird, while the band again plays "Hail to the Chief." The president and the governor step out of the audience and ask for his autograph.

"Free" Speech

THE WASHINGTON STAR / AUGUST 23, 1978

A little advertising gimmick may force the courts to face up to some First Amendment issues which they have successfully evaded in far weightier cases. Someone has invented an automatic telephone-dialing service which can be set to call every phone number, listed or unlisted, and summon people from their dinners, beds, or showers to listen to an advertising pitch for deodorants, hamburgers, or real estate deals. The general unpopularity of business and advertising insure that laws can and will be passed restricting the use of this machine. Inevitably such laws will be tested in the courts, raising the fundamental question whether someone's right to free speech implies our duty to listen or to be harassed.

The Constitution forbids the government to censor the content of individuals' statements. It does not force anyone to be a captive audience. The Supreme Court has done that, however, in a long series of cases stretching back over the years—and stretching the concept of free speech to imply a right for unwelcome trespassers to pester unwilling listeners in shopping centers or even private housing developments.

Speech has been stretched to include all sorts of harassing activity that chooses to cover itself with the fig leaf of communication—from union pickets harassing their employers' customers to Nazis harassing Jewish concentration camp survivors, as in a recent case from Skokie, Illinois. *Free* has also been stretched beyond its original meaning of "ideologically uncontrolled by the government" to mean "not costly in an economic sense." The right to use the cheapest way of communicating has repeatedly overridden other people's right to be left alone.

If getting under foot handing out leaflets to people loading or driving their cars in a parking lot is cheaper than taking out an ad in a local paper, mailing out postcards, or a thousand other ways of communicating, then any individual or institution that bars such activity, is violating "freedom." If speech isn't economically inexpensive, then it isn't "really" free. By this kind of reasoning, the constitutional right to privacy ought to imply government-subsidized window shades, since you can't "really" have privacy when the neighbors can watch everything you do at any hour of the day or night—and shades and drapes are costly.

Never has it been so easy to communicate in so many different ways with anyone who wants to listen—and, therefore, never has the case been weaker for bothering those who don't. All it takes is a glance at some of the huge newsstands groaning under the weight of an incredible array of magazines, newspapers, and paperbacks to realize that there are channels for communicating every conceivable idea and some ideas that seem inconceivable. And this isn't even counting television, citizens band radio, mailing lists, bumper stickers, rallies, study groups, lecture series, or cocktail parties. Anyone with any idea has ample channels of voluntary communication without the courts' forcing people to put up with his pestering them.

Much of what goes on under cover of "speech" is not even an attempt to communicate ideas but is instead simple intimidation and harassment. No one needs masses of pickets to convey the information that a strike is in progress. Nor are the Nazis out in Skokie, Illinois, to reason with the Jews who had survived Hitler's concentration camps.

You know it, I know it, and the Supreme Court knows it. But years of runaway extrapolations from the First Amendment could not be repudiated by the court even in a case that epitomized the absurd extremes to which this could lead. Better to be absurd one more time and call it consistency.

The automatic telephone-dialing machine puts the First Amendment question in a new framework, where the Supreme Court has not painted itself into a corner and where crass advertising evokes no civil liberties aura. This may provide a more rational setting in which the courts can again confront the constitutional question: Does the fact that someone has a right to say whatever he wants to mean that he can force others to be an audience?

Democracy—
or Judicial Ad-hocracy?

LOS ANGELES HERALD EXAMINER / JULY 25, 1979

Just one year after striking down racial quotas in the *Bakke* case, the U.S. Supreme Court has upheld racial quotas in the *Weber* case. What does it mean? That quotas are all right in a Louisiana factory, but wrong in a California university? That quotas are okay when Justice Powell is out sick, but unconstitutional when he is well and voting? Or maybe they have adopted the odd-even system, so that you can fill up quotas in odd-numbered years, but not in even-numbered years.

The truth is worse than any of these speculations. The courts have increasingly decided what social policy they like and don't like, under the thin disguise of "interpreting" the law or the Constitution.

This has become so blatant in the past two decades that leading law professors and law journals have urged the courts to openly proclaim their role as applying the "values" or "spirit" they see in the law rather than following what the elected legislators actually said. That means replacing democracy with a judicial ad-hocracy. We are dangerously close to that right now, and the *Weber* case takes us another step closer. In the long run, that may be more important—and more tragic—than anything the court says about quotas.

The Civil Rights Act of 1964 so plainly forbids employment quotas that the Supreme Court is forced to explicitly reject what it calls "a literal interpretation" of the act. Instead, it relies on what it calls the "spirit" of the law and the court's version of the "primary concern" of the Congress that passed it.

Although Justice Blackmun's concurring opinion speaks vaguely of what Congress "probably thought" when it passed the Civil Rights Act, there is no mystery about what they said. The official *Congressional Record* shows long discussions in which quotas, racial balance, compensation for the past, etc., were all rejected in as many different words, and as emphatically, as human beings could reject any proposition. The Civil Rights Act called for decisions *without regard* to race, color, or religion.

All this was said so often, so plainly, and so vehemently in Congress that even a Supreme Court justice could understand it—if he wanted to. Nor can they plead ignorance. Justice Rehnquist's dissenting opinion cites page after page of quotes from the late Senator Hubert Humphrey and many other leaders of the fight for the Civil Rights Act, saying what it did and did not mean.

The bold dishonesty of the court is underlined by their constant references to the "voluntary" nature of the quota scheme in the *Weber* case, and Justice Brennan's dismissal of all constitutional issues on the ground that the government was not involved. Yet the record shows that the so-called "voluntary" quota scheme was adopted by Brian Weber's employer only "after critical reviews from the Office of Federal Contract Compliance." Moreover, it was modeled after a plan the government had forced on another industry after a court case.

Why do courts twist words and torture logic like this? First of all, they are following "noble" policies. There is nothing like doing "the right thing" to justify lying, deception, and overreaching one's authority. Second, they do it because the rest of us let them get away with it. There is still an aura around judges, and those who agree with current judicial policies exploit that to keep the rest of us awed into silence. Any attempt to curb the power of courts is shouted down as an attack on the law.

Actually, there is no group more contemptuous of the law than the judges themselves. The law is just an inconvenience they have to evade in order to impose their lofty visions on the common herd.

As long as our anger at judges dissipates itself in words, nothing will change. Only when we are ready to act will these little tin gods pull back. The bickering in the California Supreme Court as election day approached, and the reversal of the *Tanner* decision after that unsavory episode was investigated, show that judges know when the public is fed up and ready to lower the boom.

There are many things we could do. We could put an end to lifetime appointments for federal judges, letting them know that even their vast powers derive ultimately from the consent of the governed. We could make free-wheeling policymaking an impeachable offense. Knee-jerk supporters of the courts will cry that this would bring politics into judicial decision making. Actually it would help take politics—the judges' politics and social visions—out of court decisions.

No one would want to see a simple majority of legislators able to remove a judge after any unpopular decision. But if impeachment for reversing the law by "interpretation" required a three-fourths majority, only the most outrageous distortions—something like the *Weber* case or the *Tanner* decision—would bring impeachment. It is hard to get three-fourths of politicians to agree on anything, even that the sky is blue.

Nothing human is free of flaws or dangers. The question is whether we are prepared to act to clip the wings of high-flying judges or whether we are so paralyzed with fear that we continue the steady drift into autocratic judicial government.

6

FOREIGN POLICY

THERE WAS A TIME WHEN American foreign policy meant things like tariffs or a skirmish here and there in Latin America. Our foreign policy might be good, bad, or indifferent, but it didn't make much difference to most Americans. Today, foreign policy means survival policy. In the nuclear age, foreign policy isn't really foreign any more. It is about whether this land, this people, and this civilization shall continue.

The separate issues that arise in foreign policy are no longer questions about Chinese recognition, or hostages in Iran, or the fate of the Panama Canal. They are questions about American resolve in the face of pressure. It is a question that is even larger than America, in an age when all of Western civilization depends for its freedom and survival on American military strength and political will. Image is in a sense more important than reality. Once we are perceived as so weak as to invite a major test, that is itself a catastrophe, regardless of how we respond.

Against this nuclear background, "practical," one-day-at-a-time rationalism becomes a dangerous way to resolve issues in isolation. Yet the temptation to sweep today's challenge under the rug is very great. Meeting even a small challenge is costly, both economically and politically. Even more costly is continually maintaining the military strength to deter future challenges. Costly and unused military power can always be decried as waste. There will always be other things that are needed that could have been bought with the same money.

The same could be said of the money we individually spend on locks, medical checkups, smoke detectors, first-aid kits, emergency brakes, insurance, or shatterproof windshields. Airplanes can fly without radar, and ships can sail without lifeboats, for that matter. People who pay high prices for their housing could probably get or build similar physical facilities at a much lower price in a high-crime neighborhood. Yet we don't consider any of these expenditures waste.

Most of us never receive any tangible benefits from our costly safeguards, and don't want to. Neither should we judge our military preparedness by tangible rewards. Freedom and the future of America are both intangible—yet not only real but precious.

Foreign policy is of course more than military policy. But in a nuclear age, our very ability to have a foreign policy depends on the military strength that gives us independence. Words like *hawks* and *doves* have lost their meaning. There are no hawks on nuclear war. There are just different ideas on how to prevent it. The high price of defending ourselves offers a constant temptation to substitute hopes and illusions for hard cash. Such magic words as *overkill* and *negotiation* are among the substitutes discussed in these essays.

While the grim possibility of nuclear annihilation is a new dimension in history, many of the attitudes behind our foreign policy go back in history—in some cases, as far back as the Roman empire. Much of the kind of thinking that led to World War II is very much alive and well—and vocal—on the American political scene today. These essays explore these attitudes and the actual record of what happened when they were tried before.

When a Nation's Will Dies

THE WASHINGTON STAR / MAY 6, 1978

The barbarian armies that finally overran the Roman empire were smaller than other barbarian armies that had been turned back and cut to pieces by the Roman legions in earlier centuries. The barbarians weren't stronger. Rome was weaker—and it was self-weakened. Each Roman legion was smaller than before, less heavily armed and armored, and less disciplined. The Roman aristocracy no longer provided officers for the legions. Emperors no longer led them in battle. Roman youths increasingly evaded military service. Rome's enemies could destroy it only after it lost the will to resist.

America's will to resist has also been visibly declining. We have abandoned the defense of American vessels seized on the high seas— both fishing boats and U.S. Navy craft. We have let our once superior military power deteriorate to what we now hope is "parity," as more and more of the military share of the federal budget has been diverted to welfare spending. Rome did that too—it makes politicians popular in the short run. Finally, we have advertised to the world our declining will to resist by turning over the Panama Canal under threat of violence.

A flood of political rhetoric about our "generous" or even "courageous" act cannot conceal the brutal fact of surrender to threats—a fact made plain by Panamanian dictator Torrijos, who went on television immediately after the treaty vote to announce that he would have begun sabotaging the canal within 24 hours if the Senate had not given it to him. We cannot grandly soar above all this on grounds that "of course" the United States could defeat Panama militarily if we wanted to. The question is not our ability; the question is our will. Lack of will defeated Rome, and it nearly destroyed the Western democracies when Hitler began his rampage through Europe in the 1930s.

Numerous probes of the will to resist preceded the onslaught on Rome and the Nazi blitzkrieg. Some of these probes were by small powers seeking small concessions, but what was ultimately crucial were the soft spots discovered by these probes. If we think that the Soviets were looking the other way while we paid ransom to South American countries who seized American fishing boats, while Idi Amin made Carter back down and eat crow, or while we crawled to get the Pueblo crewmen back, we are just kidding ourselves. Perhaps even more revealing was the denunciation and derision that greeted President Ford's attempt to reverse this trend by using troops to rescue the crew of the Mayaguez. Our sophisticates howled down this square man and his square decision, in terms reminiscent of the Western sophisticates of the 1930s who asked, "Why die for Danzig?

The Senate has said, in effect, that we are not about to send American boys off to die over the Panama Canal. Perhaps that is just as well, if we really don't have the determination to back them up and see it through. It may even be courageous and patriotic for a Senator to put his political life on the line by opposing public opinion, if the public itself will not be willing to pay the price of its desire to keep the canal. But if that is where we are, we need to be told that loud and clear, like a danger signal in the night. Instead, all sorts of efforts are made to conceal it, with verbal sleight of hand about our generosity or anticolonialism, or other such drivel. If our leaders' diagnosis of the public's will is wrong, we need to correct it at the next election. And if the diagnosis is right, we need to realize that far more formidable adversaries than Torrijos are likely to know it, and that the ultimate cost may be far higher than the Panama Canal.

A post-Vietnam unwillingness to get involved militarily overseas is understandable as a short run swing of the pendulum. A similar sense of the futility of war overwhelmed a whole generation disillusioned by the carnage of World War I. Young men in the 1930s openly took the "Oxford pledge" never to fight for their country. But once they saw the bombs falling on their homes, this generation vindicated themselves in the skies over Britain and on the beaches at Normandy. But a terrible price was paid by the whole world in the meantime, and it was almost too late. The timetable of a nuclear war may not permit second thoughts.

Once we have traded away enough military technology for social programs, giving the Soviets a decisive advantage, it may no longer be possible to decide that we have gone too far and turn back. If the Soviets ever get the same overwhelming military advantage over the United States that America once had over them, they can unilaterally forbid our development of the needed technology by declaring that to be an act of war. Just as they had to back down in the Cuban missile crisis, we would have to back down or face annihilation.

Mutual nuclear overkill can be oversold as a deterrent to international blackmail. Does a policeman have "overkill" whenever he faces five criminals single-handedly, just because he has six bullets in his revolver? It is problematical whether he can fire them at all, much less fire all of them with deadly accuracy. Nuclear delivery and defense systems, and their ever-changing technology, make the question much more complicated than whether our arsenal could theoretically kill every Russian five times over. Maybe the Maginot line could have killed every Nazi soldier if World War II had been fought differently, but such numerical calculations would have been small consolation to a defeated France.

Even where mutual overkill is maintained—and the neutron bomb decision (or vacillation) makes that questionable—there is mutual deterrence only as long as both sides have the will to resist, not when one side is repeatedly advertising its willingness to capitulate.

The Panama Canal Tradition

THE WASHINGTON STAR / JANUARY 25, 1978

It is the year 2000 and a high administration official is being interviewed.

Reporter: Sir, how do you answer the critics of our treaty to give Wyoming to Transylvania?

Official: I think those critics are well-meaning people with a mistaken sense of patriotism and little understanding of the realities of international diplomacy.

Reporter: How so?

Official: Wyoming is not vital to our national defense. It is not crucial to our economy. Much of it is barren land. There are relatively few people living there, and the government is prepared to help relocate them. Laramie and Cheyenne are historic places, but they have long since lost any strategic, economic, or political significance. We cannot live in the past.

Reporter: But why give it away?

Official: We aren't simply giving it away. We are negotiating a treaty with another sovereign nation—a proud nation, I might add, and we would be well advised to treat them as such. The era of big-power domination, gunboat diplomacy, and the big stick are past. We negotiate as equals.

Reporter: What are we getting in this deal?

Official: We are getting the good will of the Transylvanians and the approval of the Third World, as well as a commendation from the United Nations. We are reducing international tensions and averting the dangers of war. I think Wyoming is a small price to pay for that.

Reporter: But isn't that just saying that we are giving it up because we don't have the will to defend it?

Official: Look, American foreign policy is not a John Wayne movie. We don't have to prove how macho we are by fighting Transylvania.

Reporter: What positive reason is there for turning Wyoming over to another country? It's ours.

Official: Let's face it, we took it from the Indians. Our historic claims are questionable. The Transylvanians are questioning those claims and advancing their own claims. That's what negotiations are all about. We have had some hard bargaining sessions and we have hammered out an agreement. It isn't perfect. Neither side got everything it wanted. But that's the reality of international relations in the modern era. We can't be romantics and try to go back to the simplicities of the past.

Reporter: But do the Transylvanians have any real claim, other than the fact that they have rioted and broken windows at the American embassy?

Official: They think they do. Moreover, what may seem like mere rioting to American eyes may appear as the anguished rebellion of oppressed people, as seen through the eyes of millions of other people around the world, especially in the Third World. It also weighs heavily on the conscience of many thoughtful people in the West. There have been editorials backing the Transylvanian claims in the *New York Times*, the *Manchester Guardian*, and all the major newspapers in Paris. These are the kinds of people to whom we must look for moral guidance—not to a bunch of flag-waving yahoos.

Reporter: Critics have said that if we give up Wyoming, other nations will begin to demand other states. Won't that mean, ultimately, the end of the United States?

Official: Scare tactics have always been used by those opposed to creative social change. This administration won't dignify such demagoguery with an answer.

Reporter: What if the Senate refuses to ratify the treaty, and we keep Wyoming?

Official: No matter what the Senate does, we cannot keep Wyoming. If the Senate caves in to political pressures from misinformed people, we could find ourselves in a shooting war. The Transylvanian leaders have already told their people that they are prepared to land paratroops if necessary. We can't very well expect them to back down from that commitment.

Reporter: But the Transylvanian army is the size of a Boy Scout troop. We could stop them easily.

Official: How? Bloodshed! Gore! Maybe even killing people. And for what—mere land? Can we expect the sensitive young people in our army to do that? Let's face it, we've run out of options. We're going to have to turn over Wyoming.

Reporter: Well, I guess that's the way it is.

Official: You're damn right, Walter.

Reporter: Thank you, Andy.

China with a Grain of SALT

THE WASHINGTON STAR / DECEMBER 27, 1978

If establishing diplomatic relations with China was historic, capitulating to all its preconditions may be truly monumental in long-run consequences. The fate of 17 million people in Taiwan will be a grim prospect long after the euphoria and headline splash of Sino-American diplomacy have come and gone. Around the world, nations whose whole futures depend upon American steadfastness as much as American nuclear protection will have to reassess their situation after the president has pulled the rug out from under Taiwan.

Those applauding the decision either steer away from the Taiwanese issue or try to confine the discussion to Taiwan in isolation—as if the rest of the world could not see what we are doing.

Recognition of China is not the issue. The price exacted from the United States for a mutual benefit is the issue. Even more disquieting than that is the question of why Carter paid such a high price, and what that implies for the Strategic Arms Limitation Talks (SALT) and other matters vital to America's long-run security.

To put it bluntly, if Carter's political weakness at home needs international headline splashes at all cost, then all that communist nations have to do is wait him out to get whatever concessions they want in negotiations with this administration. Communist leaders do not have to worry about elections, and they control their own media image.

The current SALT negotiations are especially crucial after more than a decade of decline of American nuclear strength, relative to the Soviets. As of 1965 the United States had nuclear superiority, by any of the usual measures—number of missiles, warheads, megatonnage, nuclear personnel. By 1975, that had reversed. *Overkill* became the magic word that assured us that it no longer mattered. Never has one word been so repeated so insistently by people diverting resources from the military into government social programs with more immediate political payoff.

Is *overkill* the last word in military defense? Armies have always had overkill, long before the nuclear age. All the bullets, grenades, and cannons in France when it surrendered in 1940 would undoubtedly have killed every German several times over. But this theoretical possibility was no consolation to a conquered nation.

No enemy is going to stand still like a target that does not shoot back, whether in a conventional or a nuclear war. If 90 percent of the American nuclear force could be destroyed by a Soviet first strike, as some believe, then the other 10 percent has to be big enough to retaliate effectively, in order to deter the first strike in the first place. That means that the needed arsenal would represent ten times "overkill" in terms of theoretical effect against a clay-pigeon enemy. Actually, the surviving American nuclear force would have to be even larger to saturate enemy defenses with more incoming missiles than they could intercept, if the theoretical overkill is to be even adequate in practice.

If the SALT agreement unevenly limits American defense more so than Soviet attack power, it can be a prelude to monumental tragedy somewhere down the road. We have to leave our children more options than whether it is better to be Red than dead. The great question is, how far do our leaders look down the road when they act? With a new SALT agreement that Carter needs more than Breshnev does, it will be well worth looking hard at the fine print.

World War II and World War III

LOS ANGELES HERALD EXAMINER / SEPTEMBER 5, 1979

This month marks the fortieth anniversary of the beginning of World War II—the greatest carnage in human history. World War II is more than something to remember for its own sake. It is especially worth re-examining in the shadow of a nuclear World War III, from which there might be no one left.

Many of the theories about war and the prevention of war that we hear today pay no attention whatever to facts or to history. We are told that we have to avoid an arms race or the stockpiling of dangerous weapons, and that negotiation of differences is the key to peace. It all sounds plausible, but is there any hard evidence that it is true?

The Western democracies all too successfully avoided an arms race in the decade preceding World War II. Britain, France, and especially the United States let their military forces dwindle in size and deteriorate into obsolescence while Germany, Italy, and Japan built up enormous, modern military forces. The American army was reduced in size for four consecutive years in the 1930s, and its appropriations were literally cut in half in one year—while Japan was invading Manchuria, Germany was rearming, and Mussolini was preparing to invade Ethiopia. The U.S. Army was only the sixteenth largest in the world—behind Greece and Portugal. Never was an arms race so successfully avoided.

Then as now, the implicit assumption behind arms-race rhetoric has been that one side builds up only because the other side builds up. But Hitler built up his war machine while the West was channeling its resources into social programs, and Japan became a naval power in the Pacific while the United States was sinking its own warships as a contribution to world disarmament. In our own time, the proportion of the federal budget going to defense has been cut in half while the Soviets have built up a larger nuclear arsenal than the world has ever seen.

As for the stockpiling of dangerous weapons, we did so little of that before World War II that in the months after Pearl Harbor we had to use ships, guns, and ammunition left over from World War I and even from the Spanish-American War. American soldiers fighting for their lives on Bataan found that most of their mortars and grenades would not go off, they were so old. Our stockpile was dangerous only in its ineffectiveness.

The implicit assumption behind the "dangerous stockpile" theory is

134

that somehow it may go off, or cause war, by itself. But no nuclear bomb has ever gone off accidentally; it would be hard to conceal if it did. People still cause wars. Weakness has invited wars far more often than strength, from the fall of the Roman empire to the fall of Western democracies as Hitler rampaged through Europe in World War II. As our underground missile sites become obsolete sitting ducks for new Soviet missiles, the danger of war increases rather than decreases.

Finally, there is the panacea of negotiations and treaties as the way to prevent war. Plausible as this may seem, the facts just do not support it. The Western democracies were constantly negotiating with their adversaries in the years preceding World War II. The West negotiated away their own advantages and principles, one after the other, and almost negotiated away their survival. The United States was negotiating with Japan when they attacked Pearl Harbor.

Wars don't just happen because there hasn't been enough talk, but because one side sees that the other side is all talk. This is all the more likely when unequal terms are intransigently insisted upon by one side, and the other "realistically" accepts this as a fact of life to which it must adjust. Hitler was a master of this tactic, and the Soviets and the Chinese are no slouches either.

There are other ominous parallels between the conditions that produced World War II and conditions today. Perhaps the most important is that the West has lacked the will, even when it has had the power. In the early years of the Nazi regime, the Western nations had overwhelming military superiority. But Hitler shrewdly tested their will with a gradually escalating series of treaty violations and aggressions. The West's repeated yielding only led to bolder demands and more ruthless actions, until a point was reached where the West was finally forced to resist, even with the odds perilously against them.

The American military superiority in the first two decades after World War II was equally overwhelming. Yet the will has been noticeably declining in recent years, as the United States has backed down in confrontations with petty dictators who have seized our people in Uganda or our ships on the high seas, or threatened our canal in Panama. We have taken China's insistence on our severing diplomatic relations with Taiwan as a fact of life to which we had to adjust.

Part of this has been a war-weariness growing out of Vietnam, just as the West in the 1930s was still war-weary from the devastation of World War I. But along with this is the economic reality that military spending competes with spending on programs with more obvious and immediate political payoff. Both then and now, we have treated social experiments as a necessity, and survival as a luxury.

Munich and SALT

LOS ANGELES HERALD EXAMINER / SEPTEMBER 10, 1979

One of the perennial controversies is whether history repeats itself. It almost never does in specific events. Where history repeats itself is in principles, patterns, and human frailties.

With SALT II still being debated on the forty-first anniversary of the infamous Munich agreement of September 30, 1938, comparisons are inevitable. The image-conscious Carter administration has avoided umbrellas like the plague, even if the president gets soaked in a downpour. No one wants to remind anyone of umbrella-carrying British Prime Minister Neville Chamberlain, who appeased Hitler at Munich. Actually, however, Chamberlain did not take his familiar umbrella to Munich.

What he did carry to Munich was a set of attitudes and policies remarkably similar to those that have emerged in the whole SALT era, dating from the mid-1960s. Central to his policy was the notion that treaties were less costly than armaments and concessions less costly than war.

Munich, like SALT II, was not an isolated episode, but followed in the wake of a series of concessions abroad and years of neglected military preparedness at home. The Western democracies relied on the hope that amicable gestures toward the dictators would be reciprocated, or that peace-minded elements within the totalitarian camp would be strengthened by our conciliatory attitude.

Just the opposite was the case. We now know that plots were afoot in the German army to overthrow Hitler as early as 1938. But every Western concession undermined the anti-Hitler forces in Germany, whose main concern was to prevent the devastation of their country. The West, unprepared either militarily or psychologically to defend itself, reduced the incentives for a change in German policies or leadership. Hitler's success in wringing concessions from the democracies strengthened his hold on the allegiance of the elite and the masses alike. If there are peace factions in the Kremlin today, they will likewise be encouraged by Western strength and weakened by Western weakness and concessions.

In both the Munich era and the SALT era, the West began with a clear military superiority and ended up dangerously weaker than its adversary. As of 1935, the military superiority of the West was so great that

Hitler's generals feared taking on even France alone, and the Luftwaffe chief of staff pointed out that an air battle against Czechoslovakia and France combined would have "not the remotest chance" of German success.

How could the West have frittered away such military superiority, until they found themselves at Hitler's mercy when the Munich showdown came? More important than this historical question is a more current one: Why have we frittered away our military superiority in recent years, to find ourselves similarly vulnerable today?

In both eras, Western governments simply promoted welfare-state spending and withheld from the military the resources necessary to keep pace with the size and technological development of opposing forces. Chamberlain was as ruthless in cutting military budgets as he was compliant under Hitler's threats. As late as the spring of 1939, Chamberlain was preparing to deliver a speech devoted to his government's record in promoting social programs, when word reached him that the German army had taken over all of Czechoslovakia in violation of the Munich agreement. Today the word *compassion* is a magic political benediction for the inauguration of new bureaucracies, while the word *overkill* equally magically excuses all neglect of military defense.

The theoretical ability to kill all the enemy is not new to the nuclear era nor militarily relevant. France very likely had enough war material to kill every German when it surrendered to Germany in 1940. Theoretical possibilities mean nothing in the face of brutal realities. What matters is not the theoretical "overkill" we may have on the eve of a nuclear war, but how much of our nuclear stockpile would survive the first attack, and how much of the remainder would penetrate Soviet defenses. As the technology of attack and defense advances, there are changing answers to both these questions. There is no point at which we can complacently sleep behind our "overkill" the way France slept behind its Maginot line.

An ominous political parallel between the Munich era and our own is that Western governments that have made well-publicized agreements with potential enemy nations have every incentive to conceal from their own people the subsequent violations of those agreements by totalitarian powers.

Soviet violations of SALT I have similarly been shrouded in official silence, institutionally insulated even from congressional scrutiny, and downplayed when they leaked out to the press. This is not a measure of their military significance, but of the political devastation that would follow open admission that we have been had.

The same word, *parity*, has been endlessly repeated by Western political leaders in both the Munich era and the SALT era long after their adversaries had achieved military ascendance. With the same airs of sophisticated realism that we hear today, Chamberlain pointed out that parity cannot be judged by a single number, but involves many criteria. What he did not do was show how all the numbers and all the criteria put together showed any different conclusion than a dangerous vulnerability. Nor do his counterparts today.

As for ratifying totalitarian aggression, we have already given China a blank check to annex Taiwan long before they are militarily capable of doing it. They cannot embarrass Carter as quickly as Hitler embarrassed Chamberlain.

Finally, the Munich era and our own were both dominated by an anti-military psychology growing out of a previous war marked by devastation and disillusionment with the outcome—the First World War and Vietnam, respectively. Ironically, in the 1930s, the military leaders on both sides had a more realistic picture than the politicians or the public who brushed them aside. The German generals tried to caution Hitler against his adventures, and Western generals tried desperately to alert their leaders to the dangers. A French general of the Munich era said that he had not wept so since the death of his mother. In America, the army chief of staff, General Douglas MacArthur, vomited on the White House steps after an angry confrontation with Franklin Delano Roosevelt over massive cuts in the army's budget.

In the American political tradition of civilian supremacy, military men on duty are not to publicly contradict the civilian administration. In the SALT II hearings, the military leaders have given about as weak support to the treaty as they could get away with, and numerous retired military and intelligence officials have attacked it vehemently. Even the incumbent head of the Central Intelligence Agency has refused to back up the president's confident claim that the treaty is verifiable. They cannot be dismissed as "hawks." There are no hawks on nuclear war, just different approaches to preventing it.

Nothing is morally or politically more immediately rewarding than being for peace and against "militarism." But it can be a tragic self-indulgence to loftily wave aside the expertise of those who know all too well what war means.

SALT at the Crossroads

LOS ANGELES HERALD EXAMINER / AUGUST 8, 1979

The SALT II debate marks a historic decision at the crossroads for the United States. It is both a military and a political crossroads.

The American nuclear superiority of the mid-1960s became Soviet nuclear superiority by the mid-1970s, though politicians like to call it parity. The Soviets now have more and bigger missiles, more nuclear personnel, and more civilian defense. The real question is whether even our ability to retaliate will be gone by the mid-1980s.

Politically, we have gotten to this grim situation by the simple process of reducing the military share of the federal budget while increasing the share going to social programs of every imaginable sort. With the voters unwilling to pay any more taxes and angry about inflationary government deficits, the only way politicians can continue to hand out goodies is to keep cutting the military share of the federal budget. Liberal Congressman Les Aspin put it in plain English: "You've got to cut the defense budget if you want sufficient money for your own programs."

One of the great myths promoted by those who want to continue business-as-usual political spending is that military preparedness does not matter, because the United States and the USSR both already have "overkill." Theoretically, we could kill each other several times over with our current nuclear stockpiles. But wars are not fought theoretically. One of the first targets in a Soviet nuclear attack would be our nuclear stockpile. Many military experts think that the USSR could destroy the great bulk of it in a sneak attack.

To deter a nuclear attack in the first place, we have to be sure of having enough retaliatory power left in our *surviving* nuclear arsenal to inflict intolerable damage on the USSR. Moreover, the Soviets have to know that we have it and will use it. Big talk about how our nuclear submarines could destroy Soviet cities is hollow political rhetoric. If we annihilated all the cities in the USSR, within the hour there would be no more American cities either.

An all-out attack by either side on the other's cities would be mutual suicide, whether in a first strike or in a retaliatory strike. What we have to be able to deal with is a Soviet attack on our missile sites—or start thinking about surrender. Many doubt whether our submarine-launched missiles have the punch or the accuracy to take out hardened underground Soviet missile sites.

The most ominous nuclear development has been the Soviets' production of missiles far more powerful than would be required to destroy even the largest American city. No weapon is made without some target in mind, and the USSR has plenty of smaller missiles capable of annihilating U.S. cities. There is only one target that makes any sense for such huge Soviet missiles—American underground missiles in their hardened silos. That in turn means that the only point in such Soviet missiles would be in a *first strike*, preventing us from retaliating.

This is not to say that the Soviets have a timetable for attack. Military power can be decisive without ever actually being used. The Soviets had to back down in the Cuban missile crisis in 1961 because we had military superiority. In a future confrontation, the United States may have to back down and, indeed, accept whatever terms the Soviets dictate.

The SALT II treaty attempts to freeze the development of those nuclear weapons which would allow the United States to regain military equality with the USSR. It leaves the Soviets free to continue development of some of the systems they want. Now that we are Number Two militarily, SALT would prevent us from trying harder.

How could the Soviets think we would accept such a one-sided deal? Very simple. They know American politics. They know that President Carter desperately needs another international splash to bolster his sinking public image. They know that Congress is full of would-be messiahs who can hand out benefits to the faithful only with money chopped out of the military budget.

The steady shift of the military balance against the United States has alarmed enough senators to put ratification of SALT II in doubt. The Carter administration is trying to placate the Senate with its new plan to create a mobile missile-launching system to replace our stationary missile silos that are becoming sitting ducks for the new Soviet super-missiles.

It is not clear whether this latest scheme is meant to deter the Soviets or to deter the Senate from rejecting the SALT agreement. Nor is it clear how much of this new system will actually be carried out, once the costs begin to mount and present a painful choice between new taxes or a cutback in giveaways to various groups. Under political pressure, the mobile missile system could easily be scaled down to become too little and too late.

What a tragic epitaph it would be for this country that we could afford everything except survival.

140

Iran: The First in a Series?

LOS ANGELES HERALD EXAMINER / NOVEMBER 28, 1979

President John F. Kennedy said it with simple eloquence: "We dare not tempt them with weakness." This basic truth has been ignored for years, and we are now paying the price in Iran. And it may be only one of many installments to come.

For a long time now, we have been tempting them with weakness all around the world. We have repeatedly backed down, caved in, and paid transparent extortion, including the Panama Canal. We have taken the short end of unequal treaties with the Soviets and China. We have been pushed around by petty dictators from North Korea to Uganda.

We have blandly accepted insults at the United Nations and have fed our adversaries, who accept our gifts as a right to which they are entitled. We have pulled the rug out from under our friends to curry favor with our critics and mollify our enemies. These have not been the policies of just one president or one party. Many chickens are coming home to roost in Iran.

Attacks on American embassies have been an international pastime for decades. It was only a matter of time before someone decided to see just how far he could push it. Iran has succeeded in reaching a new low in relations between nations. For a government to hold another government's embassy employees hostage violates principles that even tyrants and police states have respected for centuries. The most elementary international negotiations would become impossible if the very people who maintain contact are treated as fair game to be seized or killed by the governments they are dealing with.

What is involved is not just a dispute or crisis beween two nations. What is at stake is the whole framework of rules that makes international diplomacy possible. All nations' ability to negotiate their differences—to avoid war and make peace—is being held hostage by Iran.

The shortsighted acceptance of outrages that got us here in the first place is still going strong in some quarters. There are some Americans who see the problem as simply one of what we can give the Iranians in exchange for the hostages. They ignore the devastating long-run consequences of letting a nation gain any concessions this way.

Violation of the first principles of international relations has to be made costly, not profitable. However restrained the United States must be right now to try to preserve the lives of the Americans held by Iran, we cannot in the end make it a paying proposition for governments to hold hostages.

Our ambassadors, our secretaries of state—even our presidents—have to travel internationally, temporarily at the mercy of foreign powers. If we ever open the door to such people being seized and exchanged for concessions, it will be more than a national tragedy. It will be catastrophic for all nations and for the cause of international peace. Common decency does not exist merely as an expression of some abstract notion of justice, but because we cannot survive without it.

Too often in recent years our deep thinkers have bought the idea that someone with a sense of grievance has a right to break the rules. This doctrine has left a trail of escalating disasters, from the college campus to the criminal courts to riot-torn streets and international terrorism. Once common decency is treated as subordinate to moral passions, the door is open for guilt-ridden indecision in the face of outrages, guaranteeing new and bigger outrages.

The same kind of deep thinkers see the Iranians' grievances against the shah as central. They liken the shah to Hitler or Eichmann. They seem to forget that no one seized innocent Latin Americans to force the extradition of Eichmann. Even the seizure of Eichmann himself aroused international criticism, despite his unprecedented crimes and the fact that he received a much more elaborate trial than anyone receives in Khomeini's kangaroo courts.

The question whether the shah was a good or bad ruler is overshadowed by the question whether international law shall be replaced by the law of the jungle.

142

Somewhat Deploring
Attila the Hun

LOS ANGELES HERALD EXAMINER / JANUARY 16, 1980

"We of the United Tribes face a serious crisis. Attila the Hun has been violating accepted norms of international relations.

"His many invasions, widespread orgies of pillage, rape, and slaughter of men, women, and children cannot be accepted by the world community.

"On the one hand, we find this behavior deplorable and call upon him to respond positively to world opinion. On the other hand, we cannot rush into action that would only inflame the situation.

"My delegation believes in finding some viable compromise between Attila the Hun and those tribes he has slaughtered or plundered. We think the issues or differences between them should be peacefully resolved through the good offices of the United Tribes.

"It is true that our efforts have not always met with success. The last three envoys we sent to Attila have not returned, and there are reports that they were eaten for breakfast. Still, we must persevere in the cause of peace and international order. Patience and restraint must be our watchwords.

"Some other delegations to the United Tribes have called for more drastic action and have used inflammatory language. The resolutions they have introduced would 'severely deplore' the actions of Attila the Hun and threaten sanctions.

"My delegation believes that the resolution should '*somewhat* deplore' the actions of Attila the Hun and that sanctions are inappropriate at this time. What would sanctions accomplish, after all?

"If we stop sending food to the Huns, Attila himself will not go hungry. Only the other Huns will suffer, many of them innocent people. That offends our sense of justice and the other lofty principles of the United Tribes.

"If we should take up arms—heaven forbid—whom would we be fighting and killing? Probably not Attila himself, but the ordinary rank-and-file Huns. That surely is not just, nor in accord with the noble vision that created the United Tribes.

"My delegation believes that we must never forget that the Huns are an 'emerging' or 'developing' tribe. A certain amount of turmoil is inevitable as a new tribe tries to realize its aspirations for its people.

"There are many complex issues between the Huns and the other

143

tribes. No quick or simplistic solutions should be expected. The issue is not simply the tribes massacred or enslaved by the Huns. We would, of course, like to see the massacres and enslavement moderated, or perhaps even ended. But we must recognize that this is part of a larger picture of intertribal rivalry.

"My delegation believes that what must first be resolved are these intertribal differences. Only in this context, and in the spirit of compromise, can the controversies be mediated.

"Much as we yearn for the eventual freedom of those currently in bondage to the Huns, we ask them and our fellow delegates for continued patience. My delegation believes that a one-sided resolution against Attila the Hun will only harden his position and make a peaceful solution more difficult. And peace, after all, is the ultimate objective of the United Tribes.

"Thank you, Mr. Chairman."

Neighborly Differences

LOS ANGELES HERALD EXAMINER / OCTOBER 31, 1979

A trim young man in a business suit, carrying an attaché case, knocks on the door of a modest house. A middle-aged woman cautiously opens the door a little bit and peers out fearfully at him. The man smiles.

"Mrs. Wilson? I'm Joe Denton from the Neighborhood Crisis Center."

"Oh, good. Come on in. I was afraid you were someone else."

"Thank you. My goodness, Mrs. Wilson! Why are you holding that gun?"

"I was scared. That's why I called you."

"Well, get rid of the gun. Those things are dangerous. Patience, negotiation, and compromise will solve any problem."

"Not my problem."

"Suppose you start from the beginning."

"We have a vicious neighbor who is trying to force us out of our home. He wants to buy our house at half price, so he can build himself a patio and a garage. He said he was going to kill us if we didn't get out."

"People say many things. But you're still here and he hasn't killed anyone, has he?"

"Well, they took my husband away to intensive care just a few minutes before you got here."

"What happened?"

"I don't know. I found him unconscious on the sidewalk in front of our house, and a lead pipe was lying near him. Our neighbor has been saying for weeks that he was going to hit him over the head with a lead pipe the next time he met him on the street."

"But you didn't actually see anyone hit him?"

"No, but in addition to the lead pipe attack—"

"The alleged lead pipe attack."

"—we have had rocks thrown through our windows every night, and we find garbage strewn across our lawn in the morning. And our neighbor plays his stereo full blast in the wee hours of the morning. Oh . . ."

"Don't cry, Mrs. Wilson. The only thing we can pin down to your neighbor is the stereo. Why don't we begin negotiating with him over that? Negotiation is the name of the game."

"Negotiation?!"

"Yes. We might even get him to increase the amount he will bid for your house."

"But what about all those terrible things he's done?"

"No, no, Mrs. Wilson. We can't bring all that into the negotiations. That would just bog down the talks."

"But those other things are all part of the same picture."

"No, no, Mrs. Wilson. You can't think like that. That's called 'linkage.' As the president himself has said many times, the linkage of one issue to another is wrong. Everything has to be negotiated separately."

"You mean we should just back down and sell out to stop our neighbor from bullying us?"

"Now, we're never going to get anywhere in the negotiations using emotional words like that."

"But he's trying to destroy us."

"No, he's just trying in his own way to negotiate an agreement to acquire property. We have to learn to see things from the other person's perspective. I think we should phone him right now and get discussions started."

"He's not in his house. He's out there digging a tunnel under his yard."

"A tunnel?"

"Yes. He says he is going to tunnel all the way under our house and plant dynamite to blow us out of here unless we leave!"

"No hysteria, please. He hasn't actually done it, has he?"

"Well the tunnel is about two-thirds of the way across his property, heading for ours."

"He has every right to build a tunnel under his own property, and he hasn't yet touched your property, has he?"

"No, but with all those other things he's done—"

"Now, now, Mrs. Wilson. That's 'linkage' again. We must deal with each issue separately. What's good enough for our government should be good enough for all of us."

"But I'm scared. That's why I bought the gun. I'm thinking of putting up a fence, buying a guard dog, and calling the police."

"Completely the wrong approach, Mrs. Wilson. Making a show of force will only escalate the tension and make negotiations more difficult. If anything, you should get rid of that gun—as a gesture of good will, to get discussions started."

"That sounds strange to me, but I suppose you must know what you are doing, since you work for the Crisis Center every day."

"Actually, I'm only a part-time volunteer. My regular job is at the State Department."

Cheap and Easy Policies

LOS ANGELES HERALD EXAMINER / FEBRUARY 6, 1980

You might think that doing nothing is easy. Actually, it can be very hard work. Sometimes it keeps the president and the whole State Department busy.

The hard part about doing nothing in politics is that you always have to appear to be doing something. Remember that naval task force that was ordered to head toward Iran a couple of months ago? Even the New York Central Railroad could have gotten there by now. But the task force's target was never Iran. Its target was American public opinion. Sending the ships full steam ahead was one way of doing nothing while appearing to do something.

Doing nothing in international relations requires lots of "stern warnings" about "grave consequences." It requires vague but emphatic talk about things we "will not accept"—like the Soviet troops that are still in Cuba. All this elaborate nothing is unlikely to scare foreign leaders. It may give them a belly laugh. After all, they are politicians, too, and know that talk is cheap.

Doing nothing is not something new invented by President Carter or Secretary of State Vance. They have merely raised it to the level of an art form. But there has been lots of nothing done by previous administrations. We did not lose military superiority overnight. We also did not lose it just because of shortsighted leaders, though there have been plenty of those.

The basic problem is that a significant part of American society—and especially its opinion leaders—is unable to reconcile itself to the fact that all benefits have costs, which must be paid. More land for people to live on and have a little elbowroom means less land for wild animals and a handful of Sierra Clubbers. More government benefits mean either more taxes or more inflation or both. Keeping the Panama Canal means being ready to fight for it.

No one denies this. They just evade it. People who are good at words—politicians, intellectuals, and journalists—spend a major part of their time and effort evading the obvious. Every wild-animal program on television becomes a propaganda diatribe against using the earth for people. It is supposed to be terrible that buffalo can't roam the way they used to. But there is no way a human community can exist on a piece of land where a herd of buffalo might come charging through any minute.

147

If buffalo or cougars need space, so do children packed into apartments. Maybe adults would get on each other's nerves a little less if they had more elbowroom around where they live—producing that "urban sprawl" we hear denounced so much.

One of the reasons economics is so unpopular is because it deals with inescapable trade-offs. Santa Claus has always been more popular than any economist. In the political arena, everybody wants rights, but nobody wants duties. But A's "right" to anything (housing, education, medical care) is B's duty to pay for it. This generation's right to freedom—or even survival—was paid for by men buried under a sea of crosses at Normandy and Iwo Jima. To say "Hell no, I won't go" when it comes to military service is to say you will take the benefits but not pay the price.

We can hardly bring ourselves to impose a real price, even on our enemies. Until very recently, it was considered unthinkable to stop sending food to anybody, because it would "hurt the innocent." Now, the only kind of serious action against any nation is action which hurts the innocent. Europe was freed from bondage to Hitler by dropping bombs that made no distinction between the innocent and the guilty. The brutal truth is that these bombs killed not only Nazis but German civilians, the conquered peoples, and even American prisoners of war.

Slaves were freed in the United States by four years of the most ghastly bloodletting ever seen in the western hemisphere. It included General Sherman's burning a path of destruction across the state of Georgia. The question is not whether that was nice, or even "fair" to all concerned. The question is whether that was better than slavery.

Nowadays we want to "stand up to the Russians"—but at a bargain-basement price. Politics can never rise very far above the level of public opinion. In an era of wishful thinking and self-indulgence, the path of least resistance for any administration is to speak loudly and carry a little stick.

Rewriting History

LOS ANGELES HERALD EXAMINER / JANUARY 2, 1980

Through the magic of science, a way has been found to send people back through time. The first person to be sent back in time is a State Department official, who arrives at the White House on December 7, 1941.

"Excuse me, Mr. President. I am a visitor from the future."

"Really? Then you must know that Japan has just bombed Pearl Harbor."

"Yes, sir. That's why I am here—to see if I can help you, by using our more modern and sophisticated approach to resolving international differences."

"This isn't a 'difference,' this is an outrage! An act of war!"

"Well, sir, in our times we don't say things like that."

"What do you say?"

"We deplore what has happened, but we counsel public restraint and emphasize our patience as we appeal to the other side's sense of fair play."

"I'm writing a message asking Congress to declare war."

"I know. And frankly, Mr. President, some of the language bothers me."

"Such as?"

"Well you refer to the day of the Japanese bombing as 'a day that will live in infamy.' We would consider that inflammatory language."

"It's not the language that is inflammatory. The deed itself was inflammatory. This is just calling a spade a spade."

"We try not to do that in our diplomacy. The whole point is to reduce international tensions and try to get world opinion on our side."

"How?"

"Well, we don't do anything that other countries might criticize. We even try to find something good in the other side—their religion, for example—and maybe flatter that a little, in hopes of getting them to loosen up and give us a break."

"I see."

"The key is to get international opinion on your side."

"Doesn't that take a long time—and tie your hands?"

"Well, yes, but patience is our motto."

"Does this approach actually get results?"

"Uh, well—we're still being patient."

"Do other countries take you seriously?"

"We're being patient on that, too."

"What other suggestions do you have to help me deal with the attack on Pearl Harbor?"

"Just to avoid appearing belligerent. In general, try to be a little informal if you can."

"Informal? How?"

"Well, it might have helped your image if you had worn a sweater when you were broadcasting your fireside chats from the White House."

"A sweater?"

"And there's the way you sign your name."

"My name?"

"Yes—Franklin D. Roosevelt. That sounds so formal and forbidding."

"But that's my name."

"I know. But our president is named James Earl Carter, and he doesn't sign himself James E. Carter."

"What does he call himself?"

"Jimmy."

"You think I should sign this message to Congress 'Frankie'?"

"It might help."

"You think the American people want that?"

"That is our theory."

"How often has your president been re-elected?"

"Well, that's an embarrassing question. It's not clear whether he is going to be renominated."